Country Wisdom

Gail Duff lives in Kent with her husband, Mick Duff, the photographer. She is well known for her original and lively broadcasts on Radio Medway and for her contributions to *Kent Life* and other local magazines and papers, taking her topics from all her main interests – cookery, wine-making, country life and local customs. The strikingly original quality of her personality and approach makes Gail Duff the most exciting new voice to emerge in the field of cooking and food writing. She won the 1977 Glenfiddich Award, Cookery Journalist of the Year for her articles in *Vole*.

Previously published by
Gail Duff in Pan Books

Fresh All the Year
Gail Duff's Vegetarian Cookbook

Gail Duff

Country Wisdom

Pan Original
Pan Books London and Sydney

for Vic

First published 1979 by Pan Books Ltd,
Cavaye Place, London SW10 9PG

ISBN 0 330 25663 7
Printed in Great Britain by
Richard Clay (The Chaucer Press) Ltd, Bungay, Suffolk

Acknowledgements

Much of the wisdom in this book has been gleaned from farmers and growers and other country people during the course of my work and research over several years. They may have said just the odd, interesting phrase which was hastily scribbled down, or they may have given me pages of facts and information. Those I should like to thank in particular are:

Tim Long – sheep
Ralph Stevens – apples and pears
Kevin Ferrett – cattle
Fred Scott and his workers – hops
Jack Milsted – pigs
Michael Luck – cider

The following people I have approached specifically for their words of country wisdom:

Vic Morris (my father) – country wines and beers
Ken and Audrey Beevor – bee-keeping
Anne May – dairying (cheese)
Mid Grimshaw – dairying (butter)
Ted Grimshaw – tobacco
Percy Waghorn – tobacco
Jack Temple – practical gardening
Alan Brockman – biodynamic farming and growing

My thanks to them all.

Contents

Foreword by Richard Boston 9
Introduction 13

1 On the land 15
2 The country household 65
3 Nature's way 95
4 The weather 148
5 Country fare 157
6 A calendar of country recipes 177

Bibliography 218
Index 221

Foreword

There was an old chap on the farm I was brought up on who used to tell interminable stories at every opportunity, and if there wasn't an opportunity then he would create one. Since I was an idle lad, always on the look-out for respite from whatever arduous labours my father had imposed on me, I used to encourage the welcome interruptions afforded by the rambling narratives which we used to refer to as 'long stories' – partly because they were the opposite of short stories and partly because, as luck would have it, his name was Long.

Unfortunately I remember very little of what he said, and it is only now that I realize what an opportunity I missed. I would give a great deal to hear those monologues again. For one thing Mr Long was an unusually sharp observer of natural history. He was always pointing out birds' nests in hedges which other people had passed dozens of times without noticing anything, or spotting a hare crouching in long grass, or an unusual flower. He had spent all his life in the country, most of it as a labourer on small mixed farms, working with horses, and turning his hand to anything from milking a cow to thatching a hay-rick. Since he must have been about sixty when I knew him, and since that was some thirty years ago, he contained an experience of rural England that went back well into the nineteenth century, and had an obvious eagerness and aptitude for communicating it. I often wish that my attention to his talk had been motivated more by interest and less by laziness. I could have learnt a great deal.

As it is, about the only thing I can remember him saying was something that even a person of my tender years could see at once was nonsense. It was one of his many weather rhymes, and it went like this:

When the moon is on its tip
Then it will surely drip.

This still seems to me a remarkable combination of meteorological inaccuracy and metrical ineptitude. The same is true of a great many examples of rural lore. Take the rhyme which claims to predict summer weather on the basis of which of two trees comes first into leaf:

If the oak before the ash
Then there will be a splash.
If the ash before the oak
Then there will be a soak.

Or something like that. Again, it's feeble as verse and – I say this as one who has checked the phenomenon for some years now – without factual basis.

Gail Duff has included in this book some splendid examples of this kind of thing. They are to be relished rather than heeded. I have no intention of carrying a hedgehog's skull as a way of preventing toothache: there are far more effective methods available on the National Health Service. Yet I am delighted to learn that this strange form of prophylaxis was once recommended. On the other hand another dental remedy she quotes – oil of cloves on cotton wool applied to an aching tooth – really does work.

A good deal of country wisdom is concerned with when is the right time to do particular things, in the house and garden and in the fields. In my experience the rural adage invariably turns out to mean that the correct time to have done a particular job was two months ago. More practical general advice is that the best time to carry out any job is when it is convenient to you. Otherwise you turn yourself into a slave of the seasons.

But these funny little bits of advice should not be simply swept away. Each of them is worth preserving for its own sake. In this book we are told that 'if you can sit on the earth with your trousers down and it feels all right, sow your barley and it will be up in three days'. Whoever said that was surely pulling someone's leg: there must have been a lot of chortling behind the hedge when the victim went out into the middle of a field to see if it was barley-sowing time. But at the same time many sayings really do encapsulate sound sense. 'Good fences make good neighbours' is an example. Gail Duff's collection of such adages is a judicious mixture of the trite and the true.

In addition she has collected a wealth of advice and practical tips about all sorts of home activities – from making wine, cider and beer to bread and cosmetics, and from bee-keeping to cheese-making. This is useful not only because it links us with our past but also because it is often really helpful information which has been arrived at by the collective experience of whole communities over, in some cases, centuries.

More and more people nowadays are refusing to play their parts in society as mere consumers, as supermarket fodder who will meekly pay dizzy prices for expensively packaged products that are bland and characterless. More and more people want real bread, real cheese, real beer, and other real products instead of the artificial ones that are pushed in TV advertisements and sold in chain stores. More and more people, if they can't get the real thing in a shop, will make it themselves. And they find that compared with the mass-produced commercial products the real thing, which they've made themselves, is not only much cheaper but also usually much better. Of course things can go wrong, but then there's no better way of learning than from your mistakes. What is surprising is how easy most of these things turn out to be. Just have a go: take good advice, follow the instructions, use your common sense, and the clouds of mystery that surrounded brewing or baking or whatever it may be are blown away.

Doing and making things yourself is not just cheaper and better: it's enjoyable too. Any creative activity – gardening, knitting, carpentry, cooking or whatever – is fun. Sometimes it may seem like work, but that's not a contradiction. The more that the words 'fun' and 'work', 'leisure' and 'labour' can be applied to the same activities the happier we all will be.

This book is a useful contribution to that ideal. At the same time it brings together some of the encapsulated experience of the past (that is, it's wisdom) in a way that provides practical pointers for those who envisage a post-industrial future that may well be less affluent than the present one, but need by no means be worse. On the contrary, the change from mere passive consumption to activity and creativity is one to be made not from necessity but for preference.

Richard Boston
The Old School House
Aldworth
Reading
Berkshire
1978

Introduction

What is country wisdom?

It can be found in old sayings and proverbs repeated for centuries, that came about either through religious and superstitious beliefs or through man's experience of living and working with Nature.

It forms the basis of customs observed on certain occasions and at certain times of the year.

It is in the lines of folk songs and wassail songs and good-luck toasts sung at the year's feasts.

It is in the works of farmer-writers like Thomas Tusser and Arthur Young.

It is in handbooks and pamphlets written for and by country people.

It is in recipe books and herbals.

It is in the verses of country poets such as John Clare who stood back from everyday country life and observed and recorded it meticulously and beautifully; and others like Kipling who had a feeling for the country's history.

It is in the books of modern writers who have taken the trouble to research and record details of country life.

It is an intangible knowledge and capability that is often felt by someone who comes from a long line of country people.

It is the experience that is gradually gained by one who moves from town to country life.

It can be heard in conversations in field, pub and market.

It can be discovered by asking farmers, smallholders, gardeners, bee-keepers, wine-makers, dairy-keepers or any other country man or woman about their life and work, and by watching them at their tasks.

Country wisdom is timeless, yet continually evolving.

The wisdom in this book is not mine, it is other people's – those unknown; poets whose works I have come to know so well that I feel I almost know the writers; and, most of all, friends whose experience and knowledge in their own particular fields I can never hope to match. I have simply brought it all together to produce a book which I hope is both practical and entertaining.

It has been a pleasure to write and the wisdom that I have gained has only taught me how very little I know.

1 On the land

The Farm

In the country, most of the land is agricultural, so the daily life of the countryman is inevitably bound up with that on the farm. It was more so at the beginning of this century before too much mechanization replaced man and animal power, but the wisdom of the farmer is as great now as it ever was. These sayings are a mixture of old and new.

The land is the tool of the farmer's trade.

The farmer should remember that he is only the caretaker of the land for his lifetime – someone else will be farming it after him.

The top 5 cm (2 in) of the soil are the most important – so look after them.

A farmer should live as though he were going to die tomorrow; but he should farm as though he were going to live for ever.

When you take over a new farm, don't plant anything until you have proved the land – get the feel of it, see it is in good heart and see what it is good for.

Farm in front of your rubbish (weeds).

With regard to selective or mixed farming
A farmer should diversify enough not to collapse over one disaster, but he must make sure he is master of everything.

A good farmer should always have something in reserve.

The farmer may look rich, but he has constantly to be retackling the farm. He has to buy stock, seed, equipment and machinery, and houses for his workers.

The modern farmer's job is complicated and involved. He has to have an immense store of knowledge and must care about his workers and his stock.

Trim, tram,
Such is master,
Such is man.

He who by the plough would thrive,
Himself must either hold or drive.

Good ferme and well stored, good housing and drie,
Good corne and good dairie, good market and nie:
Good shepherd, good tilman, good Jack and good Gil,
Makes husband and huswife their coffers to fil.

Ploughing
Good ploughing lies at the root of good farming.

He that ploughs deep while sluggards sleep,
Will have corn to sell and keep.

If possible, plough when the moon is in descending activity.

To plough rushes is copper;
To plough heather is silver;
But to plough bracken is gold.

Ploughing song
Broad and Beauty, do your duty,
 Chupader, woah,
Time and Reason, work for Season,
 Chupader, woah,
Young and Old, work when you're told,
 Chupader, woah!

After ploughing
If you have a good soil structure, it isn't necessary to leave the soil bare in winter for the frost to break it down.

Soil in good heart is never bare.

Dry your barley land in October,
Or you'll always be sober.

On crop rotation
Each field is an individual; change its crops and give it different colours every year.

Planting and sowing

To know when the soil is ready
If you can squeeze a handful of soil together and it sticks, it is too wet.

If the earth makes any kind of noise under your foot it will be too wet.

If you can sit on the earth with your trousers down and it feels alright, sow your barley and it will be up in three days.

Howe shall ye knowe the seasonable tyme?
Go upon the lande, that is plowed and if it
synge or crye, or make any noyse under
thy fete, then it is to wet to sowe:
And if it will make no noyse and will bear thy
horses, thanne sowe in the name of God.

Wheat and barley are sown in autumn and in spring.

Sow corn when the moon is waxing, never when it is waning.

Sow corn when the moon is in Leo.

Where water all winter, annoyeth too much,
Bestow not thy wheat, upon land that is such;
But rather sow oats or else bullimong* there,
Grey peason or runcivals, fitches or tare.

Drunk or sober,
Sow wheat in October.

Sow timely thy whitewheat, sowe rie in the dust,
Let seede hav his longing, let soils have hir lust:

* corn and vetch

Let rie be partaker of Michaelmas spring,
To beare out the hardness that winter doth bring.
Who soweth in raine, he shall reap it with teares,
Who soweth in harmes, he is ever in feares,
Who soweth ill seed or defraudeth his land,
Hath eye-sore abroad, with a coresie* at hand.

Who in January sows oats,
Gets gold and groats.

Upon St Davids Day,
Put oats and barley in the clay.

Who soweth his barlie too soone or in raine,
Of otes and of thistles shall after complain.

When the elm leaf is as big as a mouse's ear
When you sow your barley, never fear.
When the elm leaf is as big as an ox's eye,
Then say I, Hie, boys, hie!

Sowe barlie in March, in April and Maie,
The later in sand, and the sooner in claye.
What worser for barlie than wetness and cold?
What better to skilful than time to be bold?

In Maie is good sowing thy buck or thy branke.†

Change your seed evry yere Michaelmas, for it shall be more advayle for you to seede your londes with seede that growe on other mennes londis than with seede that growe on your owne lande.

Four seeds in a hole:
One for the rook, one for the crow,
One to rot, and one to grow.

or
Four seeds in a hole:
One for the birds,
One for the mice,
Two for the master.

* trouble
† seed-corn

You get a higher yield if sheep are allowed to graze the young corn.

Treading down the young corn makes it grow sturdy.

Bird-scaring

No sooner a sowing, but out by and by,
With mother* or boy that Alarum can crye:
And let them be armed with sling and with bowe,
To scare away pigeon, the rooke and the crowe.

When young children were sent out into the fields to keep the birds away from the crops, they shouted all kinds of rhymes, partly to scare the birds and partly to keep themselves company. The songs are very similar from up and down the country and differ only in dialect and turn of phrase:

And God made little boys to tend the rook and crow.

Cadows and crows,
Take care of your toes,
For here come my clappers
To knock you down back'uds.
Holla ca-whoo, ca-whoo!

Here comes a stone
To break your backbone:
Here comes the farmer
With his big gun,
And you must fly
And I must run.
Holla ca-whoo, ca-whoo!

Ye pigeons and crows, away, away!
Why do you steal my master's tay?
If he should come with his long gun,
You must fly and I must run.

Vlee away, blacki cap,
Don't ye hurt my measter's crap,

* girl

While I fill my tatie-trap
And lie down and teak a nap.

O all you little blackey tops,
Pray, don't you eat my father's crops
While I lay down to take a nap,
Shuu-a, shuu-a!
If father he perchance should come,
With his cocked hat and his long gun,
Then you must fly and I must run,
Shuu-uu-uu-a!

Shoo-hoo! Shoo-hoo!
Away, birds, away.
Tek a corn
And leave a corn
And come no more terday.

He, hi, ho, here I go, up to my knees in snow,
Girt bird, little bird, ait enough, pick enough,
My master got enough,
Home is his barley now.

Crops and weather

A light Christmas, a light wheatsheaf,
A heavy Christmas, a heavy wheatsheaf.

If the first snow fall on moist, soft earth, it indicates a small harvest; but if on hard, frozen soil there will be a good harvest the following year.

The grass that grows in Janiveer
Grows no more all the year.

If in February there be no rain,
The hay won't goody, nor the grain.

March dust is worth a guinea a houch.

A peck of March dust is worth a king's ransom.

A damp, warm March will bring much harm to the farm.

March dust and a shower in May,
Makes the corn green and the fields gay.

Dry March, wet May,
Plenty of corn, plenty of hay.
Wet March, dry May,
Little corn, little hay.

If it thunders on All Fool's Day,
There will be good crops of corn and hay.

When Aperl blows his horn
'Tis good for hay and corn.

Fogs in April bring a poor wheat crop.

If the crows stay home on Easter Day, then grubs and pests will afflict the year's crops.

A good deal of rain on Easter Day,
Gives a crop of grass but little good hay.

Better an April sop
Than a May clot.

Bad for the barley and bad for the corn,
When the cuckoo comes to an empty thorn.

When the cuckoo comes to the bare thorn,
Sell your cow and buy your corn;
When he comes to the full bit,
Sell your corn and buy your sheep.

Cuckoo oats and woodcock hay
Make the farmer run away.

Fine weather from Easter to Whitsuntide produces much grass and cheap butter.

April and May between them make bread for all the year.

Water in May is bread all the year.

A snowstorm in May
Brings weight to the hay.

A foot deep of rain will kill hay again;
But three feet of snow will make it come mo'.

Cold May and a windy
Makes barnes fat and findy.

A dry May and a rainy June
Puts the farmer's pipe in tune.

A misty May and a hot June,
Makes the harvest come right soon.

Calme weather in June,
Corne setteth in tune.

No tempest, good July,
Lest the corne looke ruely.

A shower of rain in July, when the corn begins to kern, is worth a plough of oxen, and all belonging thereto.

Many rains, many rowans,
Many rowans, many yawns.*

Haymaking

Nowadays, fields are specially sown for hay, usually with rye grass, but this is a dominant lay and will soon take over completely. It is being proved that the indigenous grasses are better for the soil. Haymaking in some areas was called the Haysel (sael means time or season).
Tedding is shaking, turning and spreading the grass out to help drying. Cocking is making the grass into piles.

The grass and the soil go together.

The grass should be
Sweet an' dry an' green as't should be,
An' full o' seed an' Jeune flowers.

Let cart be well searched without and within,
Well clouted and greased ere hay time begin.

Mow grass and make hay while the moon is on the wane.

* Light wheat grains

At midsummer
Set mowers a-mowing, where meadow is growne,
The longer now standing, the worse to be mowne.

Take heede to the weather, the wind and the skie,
If danger approacheth, then cock apace crie.*

There were once about twenty different types of haystack in England. Each stack often contained one day's carting which was left for a fortnight to settle before it was thatched. If there is too much moisture in hay, spontaneous combustion can take place. To prevent it, crossed scythes were placed on top of the load on the way home.

The last load was called the Hay-home.

A good hay year,
A bad fog year.

The farmer should always make sure he has enough hay to last the winter:
Hanged hay never does cattle.
(i.e. the hay that has been bought and therefore hung on the scales is never as good for your cattle as that grown on your own land.)

A farmer should have on Candlemas Day, (2 February),
Half his litter (straw) and half his hay.
(It was also said – two-thirds his hay.)

Harvest
Wheat
When I was young and in my mother's lap,
She never gave me milk or pap:
She never sang me lullaby,
But left me there to live or die.
Then I sprang up, became all green,
I looked like some fairy queen.
Then I turned from green to yellow,

* stop work

And I became a noble fellow.
A rub-a-rout came and cut me down,
And in a band my body bound.
Then they carried me to the barn,
There I thought I could take no harm.
Here comes a man with a stick cut in two,
Then he places me on the floor:
He broke my back, knocked out my brains,
And thus rewarded me for my pains!

Colours of the fields
Harvest approaches with its bustling day
The wheat tans brown and barley bleaches grey
In yellow garb the oat land intervenes
And tawny glooms the valley thronged with beans.

To know when corn is ready
Look to see the colour.
Check the hardness of the grain.
If you can tie a knot in the straw without breaking it, it isn't ready.

If the wheat is not ready and the weather is wet, the rain can get trapped in the ear and make the grain sprout.
The best way to avoid this would be to cut the wheat, make it into stooks and let it dry in the field, but with modern combines this is impossible.

If ripe corn is left too long it gets loose in the ear and scatters.

Traditionally, the first wheat had to be cut at Lammas (1 August); and harvest always takes place from August to September.

August
Make sure of reapers, get harvest in hand,
The corne that is ripe, doo but shed as it stand.

Now Lammas comes in,
Our harvest begin,
We have done our endeavours
To get the corn in;
We reap and we mow,
And we stoutly blow,
And cut down the corn,
That sweetly did grow.

When a combine harvester is surrounded by dust, it goes well.

We've ploughed, we've sowed,
We've ripp'd, we've mowed,
We've carr'd our last load,
And aren't overthrowed!

Storing the corn
When corn is threshed on the farm:
Gather wheat from the threshing floor in the wane of the moon and towards the end of the month; it will be dry and not go mouldy.

Corn laid up at full moon will be soft and moist and liable to crack and burst.

Apples and pears

You don't make an apple – it grows.

Setting the trees
Apples:
Sett them at Allhallow tide and command them to grow,
Sett them at Candlemas and entreat them to grow.

Who sets an apple tree may live to see its end;
Who sets a pear may set it for a friend.

Grow pears
For your heirs.

Pruning and grafting

Prune fruit trees in January and February.

Graft new branches on to established stock in March, but only if the weather is warm.

In March is good graffing, the skilful do know,
So long as the wind in the east do not blow:
From moon being changed, till past be the prime,
For graffing and cropping, is very good time.

If you graft new branches on to the base of an established tree you can very quickly change the variety of apple you grow without having to wait for new trees to become established. After three years your crop is as large as before grafting.

All Conference pears are grafted on to Quince A stock and all Comice on to Quince B. Comice grows bigger and Quince B is smaller stock. If you use pear trees the trees will be too big.

Modern grafting wax doesn't have to be heated – you can put it on with your bare hands – but it doesn't stand up to extremes of temperature. The best grafting wax is the old Swedish pitch made with tallow, beeswax and resin. It won't crack in cold weather or run in hot weather and will bend without breaking. (Elderly fruit farmer who had been using the same pitch-pot since he was sixteen)

Swedish pitch is a dark reddy-brown, soft to the touch, with a surface texture of smooth, hard, shiny rubber.

Order of fruit blossoms
plums
pears
cherries
apples

Leaf buds on apple trees should appear before bloom buds.
But if they should fruit too early:
March dust on apple leaf
Brings all kind of fruit to grief.

If apples bloom in March,
In vain for 'em you'll sarch;
If apples bloom in April,
Why then they'll be plentiful;
If apples bloom in May,
You may eat 'em night and day.

or
If the apple tree blossoms in March,
For barrels of cider you need not sarch;
If the apple tree blossoms in May,
You can eat apple dumplings every day.

Rain
Fruit trees need a little rain in June to produce a good crop.

Unless the orchards are christened on St Peter's Day (29 June) the crop will be poor.

❀ ❀ ❀

Scab
The Conference pear is a strange animal – when it does scab it really goes to town.

When Bramleys are first grown they don't scab for about twenty-five years and then they can't stop.

❀ ❀ ❀

Harvesting the crop
September blow soft
'Til fruit be in loft.

Winter fruit must be picked and stored at full moon so it will not lose its plumpness.

The best money-spinner of all crops is the Conference. The Comice is the better pear but it does not crop as regularly.

A one-hundred-year-old pear tree can yield one tonne of pears a year.

Don't waste fruit and store it well
At Michaelmas and a little before
Away goes the fruit along with the core;
At Christmas and a little bit arter
A crab in the hedge is worth looking arter.

Hops

Hops take up large amounts of land and are cared for throughout the year, but the picking season only lasts from two to four weeks at the beginning of September. Everything depends on a successful harvest.

Hops make
Or break.

Hops are a Constant care but uncertain profit.

but
If it were not for the hops,
The farmers would have to hop themselves.

Ground gravelly, sandy, and mixed with clay
Is naughty for hops any manner of way,
Or if it be mingled with rubbish and stone
For dryness and barrenness let it alone.

Chuse soil for the hop of the rottennest mould,
Well dunged and wrought as a garden plot should:

Not far from the water (but not overflown),
This lesson, well noted, is meet to be known.

The sun in the South, or else Southly and West,
Is joy to the hop as a welcomed guest.
But wind in the North or else Northerly East,
To hop is as ill as a fray in a feast.

Never refer to a hop field, it is a hop garden.

A hop plant is called a heel.

In March at the farthest dry season or wet,
Hop roots so well chosen, let skilful go set.

Unless a farmer changes the variety of hops that he grows, the heels stay in the ground from one harvest to the next. In March the first shoots begin to grow, looking like small, red asparagus tips.

If the oak is out first there will be a good year of hops.

Hop poles and wires

There are eighty-four rows of poles to 35 hectares (14 acres) of ground.

There have to be diagonal braces at the end and one row in the middle.
Overhead horizontal bracing poles at the ends of the rows keep everything stable. They stretch between the first two and sometimes the first three poles.
The wires are tied on to the second pole in, at either end.

The wires will last for years, but once one goes the lot goes, and you can hear them pinging all over the place.

Hop-stringing

Thick coconut string is tied from the top wires to the bottom ones for the hop to climb up.

48,000 Kilometres (30,000 miles) of string are used each year in Kent alone.

The string is cut on a wooden turntable known as a windwom.

With short stilts your feet are 2.7 m (9 ft) from the ground; with long ones they are 3 m (10 ft) above.

Tie the string on to the wires with two half-hitches.

There are six strings between each pole: two strings to the heel.

There are 125 heels per row.

On a good day an experienced stringer can work down one side of a row and back along the other in three-quarters of an hour, tying 500 knots.

The worst weather for stringing is a cold wind – it upsets your balance, tangles the strings and blows grit in your eyes.

I like it up here – it's nearer the sun. (Hop-stringer on a cold, windy day)

May
Get into thy hop-yard, for now it is time,
To teach Robin hop, on his pole how to climb:
To follow the sun, as his property is,
And weed him and trim him, if aught go amiss.

Diseases and pests
mildew
mould
vertecillium wilt
aphids
hop-damson beetle

Hop-picking
If hops looke browne
Go gather them down.

Hops should not really look brown, but fresh and green. Any brown ones are usually thrown away.

Picking implements
a hook to cut the bottom of the strings
a pole-pulling knife (a short, sharp knife on the end of a stout pole) to cut the top of the string

Take hop to they dole
But break not his pole

The string of hops is cut down from the wires and taken to a shed where the petals are picked off by machine.

It takes a hop-picking machine about eight years to pay for itself, as it is only used at the most for six weeks in a year.

The picking machine has cut down on the number of workers needed from two hundred to ten.

If you have a few loyal workers they will turn up in all weathers to do their stints, but in the old days very few casual pickers wanted to work in the rain and so even with all that labour around a day's harvesting was lost. (Hop farmer)

After picking
Repair the wires and poles, grub out any unwanted heels and replace them with new ones.

Hop poles preserve
Again to serve.

Hop poles by and by
Long safe up to dry.

Lest poles wax scant
New poles go plant.

Hop-drying
Pokes – the small sacks in which the hops are taken from the machine shed to the oast house.

Hops are dried in round kilns in the oast house. Hot air rises through them from the burners below.

Brimstone burned in a pan behind the burner kills off any bugs and keeps the hops fresh and green.

The temperature of the burner is 37.8°C (100° F) for the first hour and then 60°C (140° F) for up to eight and a half hours.

To tell when hops are done, rub a few between your fingers and the string (stalk) should give out no moisture at all.

Brush the hops out of the kiln and on to the cooling floor and leave them for four to five hours.

Oast house equipment
scuppet – a shovel made up of a wooden frame with a tapered edge and a piece of hessian stretched across. It is soft and doesn't damage the hops.
birch broom – small besom for sweeping out the kiln.
long broom – one large birch twig used for sweeping the hops down the cooling floor to the press.

The hops are pressed into a pocket – a long, narrow sack, stamped with the name of the farmer, which takes 68 Kg (1½ cwt) hops.

Two skilled men can press fourteen pockets per hour, but a new lad will do much less.

Hops dried in loft
Aske tendance oft
And shed their seedes
Much more than needs.

Hops dried, small cost,
Ill kept, half lost.

Hops quickly be spilt,
Take heed if thou wilt.

After picking, the oast house goes back to sleep and the fields are bare until March:
Soone come, soone go,
This life is so.

Farm animals

Despite modern milking parlours and methods of early lambing, farmers and stockmen still care for their animals. If they didn't, their stock would not thrive. Individual cows, sheep and pigs are recognized and any weak points are looked for, even though they may have numbers instead of names. Cows are looked over at milking, pigs at feeding time, and every morning the shepherd has to 'do his look'.

A good stockman always knows when something is wrong. It doesn't matter how automated you get, he still wants to look at his animals.

Whether a stockman succeeds or not depends on whether he's a stockman for his 'Friday Night' (pay) or because he loves animals.

The big advantage of a small farmer is that he does it himself and can keep a check on everything. If a big farmer's got a bad stockman, then he's in trouble.

Each farmer has his own ideas as to whether sheep or cattle are best. A sheep farmer will say: 'There's more money in sheep than cattle' and a cattle farmer will tell you the other way round. The same applies to breeds. Each farmer will tell you that his particular breed is the best and will give you sound reasons.

Whatever animal you are keeping, once you have started there is no way of swapping: you must make a programme and then stick to it.

A cow, a sow and a woman, you can learn them nothing;
A dog, a horse and a man, you can learn them anything.

but
A lady's always better rearing anything than a man is.

Pigs

As good to the purse is a sow as a cow.

The pig was once the most commonly kept animal by small farmers, and by cottagers, and pork rather than beef was the traditional fare. Pigs provided fresh meat, salt pork and bacon, lard, bristles and hides.

And he that can rear up a pig in his house
Hath cheaper his bacon and sweeter his souse.*

* salted meat

Pigs are either muck or money.

The pig is intelligent, fond of attention, and susceptible to music.

Pigs have an ability to 'see the wind'. When high winds or storms are coming they will get restless and move quickly around their pens, often squealing.

Baby pigs are very shy.

Cross-breeds are hardier than pedigrees and eat less.

Buying a pig

The cottager's pig should be bought in the spring or late winter so he will be a year old at killing time.

Feeding

And twice a day give him fresh vittle and drinke.
(Seventy-five per cent of the cost of keeping a pig is its food)

A starved pig is a great deal worse than none at all.

The cottager without milk must buy a pig ready-weaned, at four months old, and if he be in good condition, he will eat anything an old hog will eat.

Always give a new pig frizzled bacon to eat and he will be contented.

Pigs will fatten quicker on meal of barley than upon any other thing.

Take paine with they swill.
Though heating be costly, such swill yet in store
Shall profit thy porklings a hundred times more.

Pigs were once let into the woods in the autumn to feed on acorns and beech mast.

but:
Acorns make hard bacon.

The basic diet of the pig has changed little over the past hundred years.

Old formula for pig food:
Grind up 318 kg (7 cwt) barley and 91 kg (2 cwt) wheat and anything else that is cheap, and put in some fishmeal.

Bought pig food is similar but it contains additives to fatten the pig quickly.

Pig pens
Make the pens well insulated so the pigs will be warm, burn up less energy and put on weight quicker.

Full-grown pigs need big pens so they can walk sometimes, even if it's not on grass.

Clean straw is warm and comforting:
Make cleanly his cabben, for measling and stench.

Breeding
Artificial insemination is only advantageous when you have just a few sows. It is a method of bringing in new blood without buying in the boar.

January
Sows ready to farrow this time of the yeere
Are for to be made of and counted ful deere.
For now is the loss of a fare of the sow
More great than the loss of two calves of thy cow.

The piglet that suckles in front will grow to be the strongest pig.

Killing
The traditional time for pig-killing was around Hallontide (11 November) so there would be bacon, brawn and soused meat for Christmas. Other pigs were kept through the winter and killed at regular intervals until Shrovetide.

September
At Michaelmas safely go stie up thy Bore,
Lest straying abrode, yoo doo see him no more:
The sooner the better for Halontide nie,
And better he brawneth if hard he doo lie.

Pigs killed in the wane of the moon will give an inferior quality meat that will shrink in the pot.

Unless your bacon you would mar
Kill not your pig without the R.

Females make the best bacon – they tend to be longer and grade better.

Sheep

Except for New Zealand, Britain has the highest density of sheep in the world. There are 200 per 2.6 square kilometre (1 square mile). Some are bred mainly for their wool, some for meat and others for both.
The shepherd is, and has always been, one of the most respected of farmworkers and his motto, 'You got to think forrard', is a valid one whether you have a thousand breeding ewes or just a small flock of some more unusual breed such as Jacobs sheep.

Once sheep have grazed a field on a mixed farm, the next crop of corn that is set there will be a prize-winner.

Sheep are a movable dung-heap.

The foot of the sheep turns sand into gold.

The land is well-harted with helpe of the fold,
For one or two crops, if so long it will hold.

You can't be lucky with feathers and wool.

Counting sheep
Up and down the country there are different ways of counting:
Hant, tant, tethery, futhery, fant,

Sarny, Darny, Dorny, Downy, Dick,
Hain-dick, Tain-dick, Tuthery-dick, Futhery-dick, Jigger
Hain-Jigger, Tain-jigger, Tuther-jigger, Futher-jigger, Full
Score.

Ina, Tina, Tether, Wether, Pink,
Hater, Slater, Sara, Dara, Dick.

Yahn, Tayn, Tether, Mether, Mumph,
Hither, Lither, Auver, Dauver, Dic,
Yahndic, Tayndic, Tetherdic, Metherdic, Mumphit,
Yahn-a-mumphit, Tayn-a-mumphit,
Tethera-mumphit, Methera-mumphit,
Jig it.

Or, have a sheep hurdle with room for two sheep to jump over at a time. As each pair goes over, say 'you an' yar partner' and drop a tally stone into a bag. Do it ten times and repeat it for each score.

Sheep terminology
Ram or tup – uncastrated male
Wether – castrated male
Ewe – female
Teg – ewe that is having her first lambs

The shepherd's crook
The slot of a shepherd's crook must be the width of the hind leg bone of the sheep. The end must be curved outwards and blunted so it does no harm.

Sheep hurdles
There are two types of sheep hurdles, the gat and the wattle. The gat is made of ash wood and is like a six-barred gate. It is used with straw bales piled against it to make pens during lambing time. The wattle is made of woven hazel rods.

Feeding
Sheep feed on grass, hay, specially grown trefoil, rape or kale, and the ends of brassica crops such as Brussels sprouts and cabbage stalks.

Save the best hay for the lambing ewes.

Wethers fatten faster than rams.

Treatment for sick sheep
Feed a large quantity of parsley to sheep to prevent foot rot.

If the sheep has a cough, feed it the roots of Good King Henry.

Sheep ailments can be cured with powdered alabaster. This was often scraped from old tombstones in churches.

Marking the sheep
All the sheep have to be marked with the symbol of the farm. The marking paint must be of a substance that doesn't down-grade the wool.

Shearing
Two men, one man and one more
Shall sheer my lambs and ewes and rams,
And gather my gold together.

The shearing pays the shepherd.

Shearing is done in the summer, usually in June. The sheep needs the wool for warmth in winter and when it is cold it is impossible to shear as the wool stays close to the body for warmth. In summer it is 'frizzed out'.

You must not shear the sheep of its wool
Before the dog-rose is at the full.

You may begin to shear your sheep
When elder blossoms begin to peep.

Shear sheep in May and you'll shear them all away;
Shear them in June and you'll come home in another tune.

If you shear when it is cold and windy, the ewe's milk supply will dry.

Shear sheep when the moon is waxing.

How close you shear depends upon the weather: when it is hot and still you can shear close; a dry wind will dry the lanolin and you leave a stubble.

Let lambs go unclipped, 'till June be half worne,
The better the fleeces will grow to be shorne.

The money you get for lambs' fleeces, it isn't worth the trouble to shear them.

To bind up the fleeces, twist the shoulder part into a long thick twine and bind it round the rest. The markets do not like binder twine or synthetics in wool.

Breeding

Ewes yeerly by twinning rich masters doo make,
The lamb of such twinners for breeders go take.

If a ram is turned into the ewes on Guy Fawkes night, you should have lambs on 1 April.

Rammes

To increase their lusts . . . give them . . . in their pasture the blades of Onions or knot Grasse: also their blossoming in the North Wind getteth Ramme Lambes, and in the South Winde, Ewe Lambes, one Ramme sufficeth fifty ewes.

Don't put spring-born lambs to the ram the following November – wait another year. They must have bone before meat.

Lambing

Lambing is the shepherd's harvest.

You plan all year for one crop and if it is lost it is a disaster.

Leap year never brings a good sheep year.

At lambing time the shepherd has to be with his flock all the time. This meant that he could not attend church on Sunday, and, so that the reason would be known on Judgement Day, he would be buried in his smock with a piece of wool in his fingers.

The shepherd was given 'lambing money' or a bonus such as three bushels of malt, just as other workers were paid harvest money. In some districts, the shepherd was rewarded with a specially made thick pancake when the first lambs were born, called the lambing pancake.

Bring all the in-lamb ewes close to the farm buildings at lambing time so the problems can quickly be brought inside.

It is lucky for the flock if the first born is a pair of twins.

Nothing is worse to a sheep farmer than a wet lambing. You will never believe the frustration and tears that go into it. (Marsh farmer)

Cold and wet together are absolute killers.

The worst loss is usually around ten per cent.

To make a ewe accept a hob lamb (orphan) when her own has died, strap the skin of the dead lamb on to the hob and leave him and the ewe together in a closed place for twenty-four hours.

Weaning

April born lambs are weaned in the middle of July, but if you want the milk for cheese it should be done earlier:

At Philip and Jacob, (1 May) away with the lambs
That thinkest to have any milke of their dams.

Tail docking

Dock lamb's tails during a waxing moon.

Until fairly recently (within the last ten years) lambs' tails were docked with a hot, spade-shaped iron when the lamb was

between two and three weeks old.
It took two men to catch the lambs and one to dock.
The tails were given to the shepherd to make lamb's tail pie.

Now, a rubber ring is put on the tail when the lamb is two to three days old and the tail drops off naturally.

Although the shepherd takes all the responsibility for the lambing, rearing and shearing, and cares for the flock all the year round, he is still only an employee:
If I had store
By sheep and fold,
I'd give you gold;
But since I'm poor,
By crook and bell,
I wish you well.

Cattle

Cattle provide milk, cream and meat, and at one time also provided labour. There are beef breeds, dairy breeds and a few that are dual purpose. Cross-bred calves born to dairy cows are often reared for beef.

Beef cattle yield little milk, but what they do is rich in cream.

Desirable qualities in beef cattle
Easy calving.
A good food/weight conversion ratio.
They should not be affected by extremes of temperature and humidity.

Many farmers still prefer the traditional breeds
Sussex cattle are the best.
There's nothing as stupid as a Charolais.

Desirable qualities in dairy cattle
Touching the gentleness of kine, it is a virtue . . . if she be affable to the maide, gentle and willing to come to the paile, and patient to have her dugges drawne without skittishness. As a cow must be gentle to her milke so she must be kindly in her

own nature, that is apt to conceive and fruitful to nourish and loving to what springs from her.
(The latter is not strictly true today since, because calves are taken from their mothers at such an early age, a certain amount of maternal instinct has been bred out.)

Feeding

In spring the cattle are put out to grass.

Other fodder includes hay, barley straw, barley pellets or cattle cake and a certain amount of urea – a dark liquid that tastes of molasses.

Serve rye-straw out first, then wheat-straw and pease,
Then oat-straw and barley, then hay if ye please;
But serve them with hay, while the straw stover last,
Then love they no straw, they had rather to fast!

Provide ye of cowmeate, for cattel at night,
And chiefly where commons lie far out of sight:
Where cattel lie tied without any meat,
That profit by dairie can never be great.

Pinch them of pasture, while Sommer doth last,
And lift at their tailes ere an Winter be past.

In Sommertime dailie, in Winter in frost,
If cattel lack drinke, they be utterly lost.

In wet weather a cow has five mouths, for each foot destroys as much sodden grass as the animal can eat.

Cows love dried nettles (although they will not eat fresh ones) and will give more milk if they eat them than they will if fed only on hay.

Milkwort is said to increase the milk-yield.

Breeding

When a cow is being served by a bull, make a small incision in her ear or nose to make sure she will conceive. (It will take her mind off the bull.)

To prevent abortion
Let a billy goat or a donkey graze with the herd.
If a cow does abort, bury the remains beneath the entrance to the cowshed so the rest will not follow her example.
Or, bury it under the mother's stall, or hang it on the cowshed wall.

Calving
Dairy calves should be born in the spring or summer and beef cattle in the autumn.

Advantages of autumn calving
The calf grows rapidly during the last two months of pregnancy when the cow is out to summer grass so both cow and calf will be stronger.
If the calf is not born in the autumn he will have a disadvantage at shows, as the official calving year begins in September.
An older calf makes better use of the first flush of spring grass when it is put outside the following April.
By the time the calf is weaned, in mid-July, the cow will be in calf again but will not have suffered any loss of condition because of summer feeding.

Disadvantage of autumn calving
Both cow and calf have to be fed and housed all winter.

When the calf is born:
Give it a handful of salt to lick to ensure it lives and becomes fruitful.
It is bad luck to step over a newly born calf.

The cowshed
Never stand a lantern on the cowshed table – hang it from a hook. (On the table, it is said to be unlucky – it probably came about as a fire precaution.)

Muck
We clear it out and spread it where we want to spread it – otherwise the cows spread it where they want it.

Horses

Before farm machinery was invented, without horses there would have been no farms. Now there are as many horses in the country as there were in the early twenties, but although some are still used as work-horses, most are used for pleasure.

Good horse, good farm.

The man who does not love a horse, cannot love a woman.

A good horse is never a bad colour.

The number of white feet a horse had was important in determining his character. If it had four, it was expected to be an unlucky animal with a vicious temper.

One white leg, buy a horse,
Two white legs, try a horse,
Three white legs, shy a horse,
Four white legs, shoot a horse.

One white foot, buy a horse,
Two white feet, try a horse,
Three white feet, look well about him,
Four white feet, go away without him.

If you have a horse with four white legs,
  Keep him not a day;
If you have a horse with three white legs,
  Send him far away;
If you have a horse with two white legs,
  Sell him to a friend;
If you have a horse with one white leg,
  Keep him to his end.

A white flash on the forehead is lucky.

A horse in a field will whinny when others pass by, and whenever the hunt is out he will become distressed even though his handler can neither hear nor see them.

Protection from witches

For many years it was thought that horses could be 'hag-ridden' (stolen by witches during the night and ridden until they were worn out). There were many ways of guarding against it!

Hang a loop of rowan twigs tied with red ribbon on the stable door.
Hang a bunch of hawthorn on the stable door on May Day.
Hang a wreath of holly and nightshade round the horse's neck.
Tie a flint with a hole in it over the stable door.
Dock the horse's tail so the witch cannot hold on to it.
For the same reason, plait the tail and mane with straw or red wool in thirteen braids.

Feeding and keeping in good condition

To keep a horse in good health, feed him mangels.

Look well to thy horses in stable thou must
That hay be not foisty, nor chaff full of dust;
Nor stone in their provender, feather or clots
Nor fed with green peason, for breeding of bots.

General conditioners to be put in the feed
burdock, ragwort, meadow rue

For tiredness and loss of appetite
dried gentian, felwort or elecampane

If he becomes thin and has digestive troubles
nettle leaves

For curing colds and also for giving an appetite
feverfew

To keep the horse on his feed
horehound

To keep down excessive sweat which spoils his looks
dried box leaves

To make the coat shine
dried powdered tansy leaves; dried and grated bryony root; sainfoin seed; a very little she-yew that has been dried and kept under the bed for a year

To cure the fever that accompanies cracked heels
agrimony

Worms
chopped walnut leaves

Breeding
If the sun shines in a stallion's face while he is serving a mare, the foal will have four white feet.

A mare in foal should never draw a funeral wagon.

If a mare has tendency to slip her foal, let her be accompanied by a donkey or a goat.

Gelding
Geld under the dam, within fortnight at least,
And save both thy money, and life of the beast.

Thy colts for the saddle, geld young to be light;
For cart do not so, if thou judgest aright.

Controlling heavy horses

The ability to control working horses often runs in families.

The possession of the Frog's Bone was once thought essential if you wanted to exercise control over horses.

Catch the black frog with the star on his back, kill him and hang him on a blackthorn tree to dry. Put him on an ant hill so the bones can be picked clean. Go to a running stream and throw in the bones. The one that detaches itself from the rest and floats upstream will be the charm.

The Frog's Bone was usually the pelvic bone of the frog, similar in shape to the horny part in the middle of the sole of the horse's hoof. A Frog's Bone will control the frog on the hoof.

Cure the bone by boiling it with a mixture of herbs and other sweet-smelling ingredients. This is the real secret, not the possession of the charm, for horses are very susceptible to smell and can be controlled by it.

The same use of the horse's sense of smell can be made with 'drawing oils' – a mixture of sweet spices which includes fenugreek.

Rub something that smells sweet on the horse's forelock or hold it in front of him and he will come forward.

If you don't want him to go with someone else, rub it on his shoulder – he will look as if he is going forward and then stop and throw his would-be new master into confusion.

'Stuff' has the opposite effect and can make the horse stay still. It is made up of oils and herbs that have a smell unpleasant to horses.

Horse brasses

Horse brasses were originally worn to drive away evil spirits and to bring good luck to the horse. Now they are worn for decoration but the old designs are still used. Some are abstract patterns and some are figures.

The crescent moon represents the Roman goddess, Diana, who was associated with horses.

The sun or circle represents the wheel which was derived from the rayed sun.

The heart was used by ancient Egyptians to protect the horse's owner.

The bell is to make a noise to frighten away evil spirits.

Pictures of crops grown on the farm are worn, in particular the wheatsheaf.

A brood mare wears a Pelican in her Piety – the pelican tearing at her own breast to feed her young.

Peacocks bring luck to the mare in foal.

If the farmer lives and works with Nature, he can be one of the most contented of men:

Let the wealthy and the great
Roll in splendour and in state,
I envy them not, I declare it.
I eat my own lamb and my chicken and ham,
I shave my own fleece and I wear it.
I have lawns, I have bowers,
I have fruit, I have flowers,
The lark is my morning alarmer.
So jolly boys now, here's good speed to the plough,
Long life and success to the farmer.

The dairy

Lately, we seem to be growing tired of factory-made cheeses and backyard dairying is becoming popular again.

Now some may drink old vintage wine
To ladies gowned in rustling silk,
But we will drink to dairymaids,
And drink to them in rum and milk.

The yield is greater and the milk richer and sweeter in summer when the cow is feeding on fresh grass.

From April beginning, till Andrew be past, (30 November)
So long with good huswife, hir dairie doth last.
Good milchcow and pasture, good husbands provide,
The resdue good huswives knows best how to guide.

13 May was the traditional day for turning cattle into the fields in Hertfordshire, and then dairywork started in earnest.

Fine weather from Easter to Whitsuntide produces much grass and cheap butter.

Milking

Fingers milking:
Ink, ank, under the bank,
Ten a-drawing four.

A three-legged milking stool should have one long leg so it tilts slightly forward. A four-legged stool should have two long and two short legs.

A cow should always be milked clean.

The 3 dl (½ pint) that comes out last has twelve times as much butter in it than that which comes out first.

If you do not milk clean, the cow will give less and less milk and become dry much sooner than she ought.

Dip your hands in warm water before milking.

If you spill drops of milk on the legs and feet of the cow, she will become dry. (A threat to make sure that milk-maids milked cleanly into the pail.)

Never milk a cow that is going to market.

The milk can sometimes 'go up into the horns', when you have to take the milk from the cow instead of her giving it to you.

A new face in the dairy can sometimes lower the yield. Sing to the cow as you milk her to bring it up again.

Hedgehogs sometimes get there before you and steal the milk from cows and goats.

In the dairy

Kepe dayry house clenely, kepe pan swete and cold,
Kepe butter and cheese to look yellow as gold.

Though cat (a good mouser) doth dwell in a house,
Yet ever in dairie have trap for a mouse.

Behave quietly in the dairy and do not slam the door for milk likes peace and will curdle if disturbed.

Soap should not be used in the dairy as its scent contaminates the milk. Rub your hands and arms under the cold water tap before you start work.

A dairywoman's hands should be smooth as butter, white as milk and cool as spring water.

Goose grease and fine lard were once the only creams permitted in the dairy for the dairymaid's hands and the churn fitments.

Dairy utensils can be cleaned with chopped nettle leaves.

The milk
The richest milk of all is the first milk that comes from the cow after she has calved. It is called beestings. It is lucky to give a little as a present to a friend, but the container should be returned unwashed to bring luck to the calf. The calf should really have all the beestings to himself as it contains substances which will build up his resistance to disease.

At one time milk from red cows was thought superior to that from those of any other colour and was specially prescribed.

Milk will sour more quickly in thundery weather.

Your nose is the most reliable guide when it comes to milk quality. The off-flavour of milk caused by disease develops after it has been standing for a few hours and an experienced nose can detect it more quickly than scientific tests.

Cover up milk and cream bowls in case a hedgehog comes to the dairy for his supper.

Butter
Come, butter, come,
Peter stands at the gate,
Waiting for a buttered cake,
Come, butter, come. (Old charm to make the butter 'come' quickly)

Butter is much yellower after the calf and also in the summer when the cow is feeding on fresh grass.

Carrot juice and marigold flowers can be used to colour winter butter.

If the cow eats putrid leaves of cabbage and turnips the butter will be offensive.

4.5 litres (1 gallon) of cream makes 1.4–1.8 kg (3–4 lb) of butter.
To 4.5 litres (1 gallon) of cream put in as much salt as will fit on the palm of your hand.

Butter takes longer to come if the cream is too hot or too cold. 18° C (65° F) is ideal.

Warm the churn and the beater with warm water before you put in the cream.

If you leave in just the right amount of buttermilk the butter will taste like sweet cream, but if you leave in too much it will quickly become 'cheesy'.

Buttermilk is the liquid left in the churn after the butter is made. Drink it fresh and never refuse it if it is offered, for fear of offending.

Use surplus buttermilk to make bread and scones.

Butter for selling commercially is made into oblongs for easy stacking.

For home use or for selling privately it can be made into any shape, but the round is the most popular. Stamp it with a wooden pat bearing the emblem of your farm or dwelling. Pictures on butter pats include a prize-winning cow, a wheatsheaf or a bird; or something to tell of the location of the farm – rushes or a swan for a valley-farm, hill flowers for a hill-farm, or the farm gate.

Cheese

Ill huswife unskilful to make her own cheese,
Through trusting of others hath this for her fees.
Her milk pan and creme pot, so slabbered and sost,
That butter is wanting and cheese is half lost.

Where some of a cow do raise yearly a pound,
with such seely huswives no penny is found.

Synchronize cheese-making with bread-making so you can use the whey and nothing will be wasted.

Cheese made in spring and summer is better than that made in autumn and winter as grass is better than hay.

You can't make good cheese with what is left after the butter has been made.

The dairy, or other room, in which the cheese is made, should be neither too hot nor too dry.

Never handle fruit before making cheese. The natural yeast on the skin will cause the milk to ferment and the curds will rise in the mould instead of sinking.

Nettle juice or a decoction made by boiling nettles in salt water make a substitute for rennet. (This was used for both Double Gloucester and Cheshire cheeses.)

Goats rue will curdle milk
In the northern counties they use this herb for making their cheeses, instead of rennet, whence it is also called Cheese-rennet: the flowers contain an acidity which may be got by distillation.

Ladies bedstraw has been used as a rennet substitute and also as a colourant.

Marigold petals will colour cheese orange.

For soft cheese it is better to use the previous evening's milk that has been standing overnight in a cool place.

Wrap soft cheese in rushes.

Methods used to make the cheese blue
Dip harness leathers or old boots in the milk churn or leave them in the dairy.
Leave mouldy bread and cheese near where the cheese is stored.

Store cheese in a cool, airy place.

Hang corn mint where the cheese is stored to prevent it going mouldy or turning sour.

If a mould starts to develop on a maturing cheese, wipe it with a damp cloth, squeezed out in cold water and put the cheese into a cooler place.

Ten guests unsent for (in the cheese):
Gehezie, Lot's Wife, and Arguses eyes,
(white and dry, too salty, full of holes)

Tom Piper, Poor Cobler, and Lazarus' thighs,
(swollen, tough, spotty)
Rough Esau, with Mawdlin, and Gentils that scrall,
(hairy or mouldy, full of whey, maggots)
With Bishop that burneth, thus know ye them all.
(scalded pan).

Chese . . . oughte not to be tough nor brutell; it ought not to be swete nor sowre, nor tart nor salt, nor too fressche . . . it must be of good savour and taledge.

Poultry

Chickens

The sound of chickens gently clucking round their run evokes all the peace of a country summer afternoon. Advice about chickens is the same if you look at the works of early writers, those of William Cobbett written later in the nineteenth century, or if you ask the advice of anyone today who keeps free-range hens.

A hen must be . . . a painefulle layer, a willing sitter; and above all things loving and kind to her broode.

Laying hens should not be old hens. Up to two years is best for a laying hen.

Let a hen lay for two seasons and then sell her for the pot.

After three years a hen will be a bad layer and tough in the pot.

No hen is worth keeping unless it can lay four eggs a week.

Even the best hens rarely lay more than six eggs a week.

Hens lay more in summer than in winter.

Let there be pins stucken in the wals so that your Poultry may climb to their Pearches with ease.

Fumigate the hen-house regularly by burning dry herbs, juniper or cedar wood.

If well fed and kept perfectly clean, fowls will seldom be sick.

Feed chickens carraway bread so they won't stray.

Add chopped nettle leaves to the feed to keep chickens healthy.

If a chicken should get croup, feed her rue leaves.

Whole egg shells should never be fed to hens.

Don't let the hens out of the henhouse before eleven-thirty in the morning or they will lay all over the place.

Some hennes by the cackling tell you when they have laid, but some will lay mute, therefore you must let your owne eye be your instruction.

Always collect eggs before sun set.

Gather your eggs up once a day and leave in the nest but the nest egg.

Very small eggs containing no yolk are called 'cock's eggs'. It is unlucky to bring them into the house.

Always put an odd number of eggs under a broody hen – thirteen is the best.

Monday was thought to be the best day to set a hen to be sure of a good hatch.

Mark a cross on each egg to make sure you know the hen turns them daily. (This could also have been a way to keep out the Devil.)

Never eat a hen mauled by a fox.

A whistling woman and a crowing hen,
Will bring Old Harry out of his den.
(Crowing hens were once destroyed immediately as they were thought unlucky and even a death omen.)

Ducks
Young ducks should be fed on barley meal or curds and kept in a warm place at night.

Grown ducks should eat grass, corn, white cabbages and buckwheat.

Ducks won't lay until they have drunk lide (March) water.

Geese

Geese can be kept to advantage only where there is plenty of green grass.

One goose eats as much grass as one sheep.

To fat a goose, feed him corn or boiled swedes, carrots, white cabbages or lettuce.

A broody goose must be well and regularly fed.

Cleavers (goose grass) should be fed to newly hatched goslings.

Candlemas Day,
The good housewife's goose lay.
Valentine's Day,
Yours and mine may.

Beekeeping

Bees, oh bees of Paradise,
Does the work of Jesus Christ,
Does the work which no man can.
God made bees and bees made honey.
God made man and man made money. (Bee wassailing song)

You should always treat bees as though they were people who would be offended if their feelings were not considered.

Bees have always been held in great respect and in medieval times they were considered holy. Legend had it that they softly hummed the hundredth psalm on Christmas Eve: 'O make a joyful noise unto the Lord.'

Buying bees

Always buy a new hive in spring. If you buy it in the autumn or winter, you won't be able to see the bees or to look inside the

hive to check for disease, so you may be getting a pig in a poke. You won't even know whether the hive has a queen.

If you buy bees in winter pay only as much as the hive alone is worth.

Barter was often the best way of acquiring goods in the country and, instead of paying for a swarm of bees with money, they were often exchanged for a sack of wheat or flour.

Location of the hive

But buy them not too far out of their air,
For change of air will put them in despair.
(This is not altogether true, but bees do take a certain time to get themselves reorientated. If the weather is good and the nectar flowing this could be as little as twenty minutes.)

Place hive in good ayer, set southly and warm.

The hives thou set a little space asunder,
Their enter, turn thou fair upon the south.

Put bees in a sheltered, sunny spot with easy access.

Avoid places that have been or will be sprayed with chemical fertilizers and pesticides.

Set hive on a plank (not too low by the ground),
Where herbe with the flowers may compass it round:

And boordes to defend it from north and north-east,
From showers and rubbish, from vermin and beast.

Predators

The worst predator is the mouse who gets into the hive in winter and eats the comb. All the while it is cold the bees cannot get to him, but as soon as it warms up they will kill him and embalm him in propylis (an antiseptic kind of 'bee-glue' with which they cement the hive).

Woodpeckers make holes in the sides of the hive and eat the bees.

Tits tap on the top of the hive and when the bees come out to investigate they fly down and eat them. For this reason they were once referred to as 'bee-birds'.

How to treat bees

If you get frightened when you are working with bees they will sense it and sting you.

Once they've got you on the run, they will keep you on the run.

Walk away and take a few deep breaths to calm yourself down, go back quietly and their anger will stop.

An old saying goes that bees will not stay with a quarrelsome family:
Quarrelsome people emit disruptive feelings and the bees will sense them and be angry and difficult to handle.

Never get angry or use bad language in front of bees.

Bees do not recognize their master as such, but they recognize feelings.

If bees have a new owner who treats them as well as the old they will not be upset. A new owner who is frightened or jumpy will displease them.

An experienced bee-keeper can tell the mood of the bees without looking into the hive.

Bees let you know – you feel how they react.

Bees do not like strong smells – they object to hair-oil, after-shave, camphor or soap.

Bees dislike strong animal smells such as those of horses or goats. Do not handle these animals before going to the hive.

Don't wear wool when you are dealing with bees as they catch their feet in it.

Don't wear dark colours as they are foreboding and the bees will attack them.

The best clothes to wear when working with bees are white cotton overalls, a plastic helmet with a veil, and white cotton gloves.

Telling the bees

Marriage, birth or buryin',
News across the seas,
All your sad or merryin'
You must tell the bees.

If you don't they will pine away and die, or swarm and fly away.

A modern bee-keeper, however, says: 'If you really had to tell the bees, I'd be out of business.' (He has acquired many of his hives from people who have died.)

The underlying wisdom of the telling lore is that at one time the owner of the bees was the only one experienced and knowledgeable enough to be able to handle them properly. When *he* died they were neglected and so *they* died, perhaps in the winter through lack of food or through disease, not as was once believed through pining away. Bees swarm whether their owner is alive or not. If he dies and no one notices that they swarm they will not be collected and naturally will fly away to start another colony.

Swarming

When bees swarm, a new queen is being reared inside the hive and the old one goes out with the swarm.

If left to their own devices the swarm will eventually find a new hive or a hollow tree.

To attract a swarm to a hive, leave an old piece of comb inside.

To make a swarm go to one of the old wicker bee-skeps, the inside was rubbed with sweet herbs and flowers such as elder flowers, garden mint or corn mint.

To rub the bramble platted hives
Fennels, thread leaves and crimpled balm
To rub the new house of the swarm.

Lemon balm grown near the hives 'causeth the bees to keep together, and others to come with them'.

To catch a swarm of bees, get a clean box and get as many bees inside as you can. If you get the queen, the rest will automatically follow.

While the old dame enjoys the sight
And raps the while the warming pans
A spell that superstition plans
To coax them in the garden bounds
As if they loved the tinkling sounds.

The old custom of 'tinging the bees' (following the swarm, banging two metal objects together) was also a method of claiming the swarm and demonstrating what you were doing so you could, if necessary, go over someone else's land to catch them:
If you ting them
You may follow them.

It was also said that if a swarm of bees settles on your land you have the right to take it.

No swarm is worth more than four pence until it has settled for three days: a day to find a place, a day to remove them, a day to rest, and all the time in serene weather.

May
Take heede to thy bees, that are readie to swarme,
The losse thereof now is a crownes worth of harme:
Let skilfull be readie and diligence seene,
Least being too careless, thou losest thy beene.

A swarm of bees in May
Is worth a load of hay;
A swarm of bees in June
Is worth a silver spoon:
A swarm of bees in July
Isn't worth a fly.

or
A swarm of bees in May
Is worth a cow and lamb same day.

or
A cow and her calf and a load of hay.

The earlier the bees swarm and start a new hive, the more honey there will be to gather in September.

Feeding the bees
21 September is St Matthews Day and on or around that date the bees stop going out for nectar:
St Matthew, brings on the cold dew.
St Matthee, shut up the bee.

During the winter the bees' food supplies become very low. They always have a store of honey but this is saved for the young bees.

December
Go look to thy bees, if the hive be too light,
Set water and honie, with rosemary dight
Which set in a dish full of sticks in the hive,
From danger of famine yee save them alive.

Bees should be fed not on set days but when the cells look empty.

Bees usually need three winter feeds: one at the beginning, one in the middle and one at the end of winter.

From this probably came the saying that bees must be given a present on New Year's Day as this is about the time of the second feed.

Bees were once fed on honey (and occasionally even on old ale), but the food which gives them the least work is sugar syrup made with 1 kg (2 lb) of sugar per 6 dl (1 pint) of warm water.

Searching for nectar

On 12 March, St Gregory opens the flowers for the bees; on 21 March, St Benedict calls them forth for their year's garnering.

Plants that attract bees to the garden
lemon balm, hyssop, melilot, sage, fragrant thymes, buckwheat.

Thyme is the plant most loved by bees.

There is little nectar around in winter, but when it is there in the summer months but does not flow, the bees get angry. (This can happen in hot, dry weather.)

The best days for nectar are high in both temperature and humidity.

No flower makes a better honey than another: it varies every year according to the weather at flowering times.

The best flower for honey is the one that fills the comb.

Some people prefer White (or Kentish) Clover honey – it is light and delicate and a pale amber colour.

Heather honey is dark and stiff with a strong flavour.

Most honeys are made from a mixture of spring and summer flowers.

The bees start gathering in spring from the early fruit blossoms and other trees such as sycamores, chestnuts and lime

The first flower is clover, and in July there are roses, blackberries and willowherb. In the autumn there are the flowers of ivy.

Honey made from rape and other brassicas granulates quickly and hasn't a good flavour.

When collecting pollen
Where they begin they will make an end: and not meddle with any flower of other sort, until they have their load.

The products of the hive
Take in due season wax, honey and swarme.

Honey is Nature's sweetener.

Honey should be taken from the hive on St Bartholomew's Day (24 August). St Bartholomew is the patron saint of bees.

This is right in the middle of the extracting season which usually starts in late June and goes on until the end of September.

The best honey was once thought to be 'virgin honey' taken in September from bees that had swarmed in May. This was true when the old skeps were used, as it came from a new comb. It makes little difference now as the brood chamber in modern hives is kept separate from the honeycomb.

When collecting honey, burn rotten elm in the smoker when you separate the bees from the honey compartments.

Take the frames of honeycomb from the hives with a hive tool. This is a flat, stainless steel implement, about 25 cm (10 in) long with a hook on one end and an oblong shape on the other.

Each hive yields an average of 13·5 kg (30 lb) honey per year.

The produce of a good beehive is worth about two bushels of good wheat.

Beeswax can be made into candles which perfume the room and hum gently as they burn.
It is also made into polish, cosmetics and medicinal products.

Propylis (the antiseptic 'bee-glue') is gathered by the bees from the sticky buds of cherry poplar and chestnut. It is a natural antibiotic and if you have a sore throat put a piece on the roof of your mouth and hold it there until it melts. (It will take some time.)

2 The country household

The house

Building and protecting the house

Nowadays, houses are mostly built for us, but if you are able to design and choose the site for your new house and build it yourself, there are a few pieces of advice to be found in country lore.

Where to build

Sandy ground is more stable than clay.

Build a house to face the south.

Catch as much sun through the windows as possible.

When building, avoid places near gallows, sites of murder and suicide.

In Dartmoor, if a man could erect a cottage between sunrise and sunset and have a fire burning on the hearth, he had a legal right to live there.

Start to build a house at new moon.

If you have to clear the site or have to pull an old house down first, do it at full moon.

When you have chosen your site, pour beer on it to prevent accidents happening during the building.

Insulating

Oat husks or walnut shells between the floorboards will insulate and soundproof.
Walnut shells serve a double purpose – they symbolize the

consecration of the marriage and the protection of the resulting family.

Thatching

Thatching was once the cheapest form of roofing, as the materials could always be bought or gathered nearby and there was always a skilled thatcher in every district. Availability of materials dictated the type and style of thatching in each county and so you could tell where you were just by looking at the roofs of the houses. Now, because of the lack of skilled workmen, the thatched roof has become the most expensive – but it is still the most attractive.

Thatch provides a quiet stillness and softens the sound of falling rain.

Thatch keeps the house cool in summer and warm in winter.

Types of thatch
Norfolk reed is the best and lasts fifty to sixty years.
Combed wheat reed (also called unthreshed wheat straw or Devon reed) lasts thirty to forty years.

Long straw lasts ten to twenty years.
Other materials include rye straw, ling heather, gorse and broom.

It is no good fireproofing existing thatch – treat the straw or reed before you put it up.

A good thatcher will not use cracked straw.

The best days for thatching are dry and sunny, or slightly humid.

On a windy day, it is more difficult to thatch with straw than reeds.

Never strip more of the roof than you are likely to rethatch the same day.

Painting the house

If the woodwork is cracked but still sound, with no woodworm or dry rot, fill the cracks with putty:

Putty and paint
Will deceive a saint.

Paint brushes for the outside walls of a house can be made from marrum grass.

Protecting the house from thunder and lightning

Storms were once greatly feared in the country for if lightning struck a wood-timbered or thatched cottage, everything was lost. Many precautions were taken to safeguard the house.

The wrought iron S and X shapes often seen on the sides of old cottages had a double purpose. A tie rod went between them which helped to prevent an outward thrust of the walls; and they also acted as lightning conductors. The S shape represented Jove's thunderbolts and the X or swastika, the hammer of Thor.

Scratch three zigzag lines on one brick to keep lightning away.

Plants and trees which helped to avert lightning
Houseleek, stonecrop or fern growing on the roof.
Bay or elder trees growing just outside the house.
An oak tree planted near the house to attract the lightning to itself.
A bunch of hawthorn gathered on Palm Sunday or Ascension Day and placed in the rafters by someone outside the family.
Marsh marigold hung, stalks uppermost, on the house on May Day protects the house from May storms.

If lightning does strike and the house burns down, it is unlucky if it does so at the wane of the moon; but if it happens in the waxing moon you will have good luck and prosperity in the future.

Protecting the house from witches
The fear of being bewitched or of being overlooked by the evil eye was, until recently, in the country a very real one. As many, or more, precautions were taken as those against lightning.

The power of the witch could enter the house through the door or the chimney and both had to be protected.

The step-like protrusion which is often found near the top of the chimney in old houses is called the witch seat, and it was hoped that if it were provided the witch would not come down any further.

Rowan trees combatted evil and a witch post of rowan was often built into the hearth or was made one of the supports of the lintel beam of the door.

Rowan, birch, May blossoms and cowslips were hung over the door on May Day to keep witches away; or on May Eve a cross of rowan and birch was put there and left for a year.

Elder leaves were fixed to the doors on May Eve and sometimes the hearthstone and doorstep were decorated with a dye made from elder leaves.

Holly and bay were hung on the door at Christmas so that the witch would stay outside counting the berries.

Iron will protect you from witches. A horseshoe hung over the door, right way up to keep in the goodness, will keep them at bay. Turn it every May morning without letting it touch the ground.

Horse brasses hung over the fireplace or built into the brickwork are a protection. So is a poker leaning against the grate.

Witch bottles containing nails, pins, needles and urine were buried top downwards in the hearth or under the threshold.

Witches hate salt. Put salt-glazed bricks in the chimney and a jar containing salt, nails, pins and needles into the pantry to protect the food.

Flowers that will protect the house from witches
St John's wort and mugwort gathered on St John's Eve
May blossom and cowslips gathered on May Day and hung over the door with birch and rowan twigs
creeping cinquefoil
basil
hyssop
periwinkle
rue, the herb of grace – rub all the floors of the house with it and witches will fly

Therewith her vervain and her dill,
That hindereth witches of their will.

Moving into a new house
Always leave a penny in the old house to bring good luck to the new occupants.

Move into a new house at new moon.

By tradition, a box of coal and a plate of salt should be the first things taken into a new house.

More practically, take a bag of cleaning materials and a barrel of cider.

Hearth and home

It is difficult to imagine how to live without such things as electricity and modern cleaning materials, but with power cuts and shortages looming in the background it is worth knowing how to manage with the raw materials of the country.
Some of the sayings relating to housework might look at first like pure superstition, but when you think about some of them you realize that they were probably originally thought up for a reason. To tell a girl that it was unlucky if she mended her

clothes when she was still wearing them was just another way of teaching her how to do things properly; and the housewife who said you would have bad dreams if the beds were turned on Friday or Saturday knew that these jobs are best done at the beginning of the week.

The fire

The heart of the home is the fireplace.

Make a fire swiftly.

All you need to look after a fire are a poker and a shovel and a thick glove for shifting a log.

Lay wood upright and it will burn fast; lay it flat and it will glow slowly.

Never burn elder wood as it spits and can be dangerous. (Once the spitting was thought to be the Devil being drawn down the chimney)

Chestnut does not make very good fuel as it smoulders and sparks instead of burning clean.

Of all the trees in England,
Her sweet three corners in,
Only the Ash, the bonny Ash,
Burns fierce when it is green.

Burn ashenwood green,
'Tis fire for a queen,
Burn ashenwood sear,
'Twill make a man swear.

Birch makes good firewood as long as it is dry.

Light, loose peat burns bright and fast; dense peat smoulders and lasts longer and gives a gentle heat.

Difficulty in kindling the fire is a sign of anger.

A flake of smut on the bars of the grate means a stranger is coming into the house. If it burns brightly, he will bring good news; if it smoulders it will be bad.

If you poke the fire and it burns brightly, your sweetheart is in a good temper.

Never waste heat
On St John's Day (19 March)
Fling warming pan away.

Cats

There was always a household cat to sit by the open fire.

A cat born around Michaelmas is called a blackberry cat and is always mischievous.

May kittens never thrive, or if they do they bring snakes and worms into the house.

Never turn a strange cat away from the door.

A cat fed regularly makes the best hunter because it hunts for sport, and, not pressed by hunger, will watch the same spot for hours. A starved cat which hunts for food eats the first prey it catches, gorges itself and lies down to sleep.

Lighting

Never waste candles, and during the spring and summer stop using as much artificial light as possible.

St Mary blows out the candle (25 March, Lady Day)
St Michael lights it again. (29 September, Michaelmas)

On Candlemas Day
Throw candle and candlestick all away.
(This is really a little too early – 2 February!)

Much spice is a thief, so is candle and fire.

Provide for thy tallow ere frost commeth in,
And make thine own candle ere Winter begin.

Myrica gale, boiled in water, makes a scum similar to beeswax that can be made into candles.

To make rush lighting

Cut rushes when they are fully grown but still green.
Cut off both ends, leaving the centre part about 45 cm (18 in) long.
Peel the green skin from four-fifths of the end.
Melt some grease (you can use the skimmings of the bacon pot but mutton fat is best as it dries hardest and burns cleanest. Beeswax added to the mutton fat makes it burn extra bright).
Soak the rushes in the grease and take them out to dry hard. Do this several times.
Lay the rushes on a piece of bark from a young tree. Anchor them in tightly.
Fix the bark to the wall so it makes a holder for the rushes as they burn.

Cleaning, sweeping and polishing

A cobweb in the kitchen
And footmarks on the step,
Find no wood in the oven
And no coals in the skep.

Of all thynges let the buttery, the cellar, the kitchen, the larderhouse, with all other howses or offyces, be kept clene, that there be no fylth in them, but good and odyferous savours.

Housework should always be done as early as possible.

Count labour halfe wonne
That early is donne.

Some works in the morning may trimly be done
That all the day after can never be wonne.

When sweeping upstairs, the dust must always be carried downstairs before noon. (It was said to be bad luck to do it after but it was a good way of getting things done early.)

Housework has always been woman's work
Sweepinge of howses and chambres ought not to be done as any honest man is within the precyncts of the house, for the dost doth putryfy the ayre making it dense.

Brooms
Make your besom from ling, birch or marrum grass and the handle from a small sapling of ash or beech.

Never leave a besom standing on its head or it will bend and become useless.

Never buy a broom in May
For it sweeps all luck away.

Always sweep something into the house for luck with a new broom, before you sweep anything out.

To sweep carpets clean
First strew them with clean grass clippings or with snow.

To scour floors and tables
Use chloride of limewater and silver sand.

Where the floor is greasy use Fuller's earth and soap.

Tough scouring be needful, yet scouring too much
Is pride without profit, and robbeth thy hutch.

Before polishing wood floors
Rub soft leaves into them to stain them.

To polish red tiles
Use the stems, leaves and flowers of red raddle.

If beeswax is too expensive
Use hot vinegar and water to wash polished furniture; or stain it brown with strong beer.

To clean pewter
Rub it with fine bath-brick that has been sifted through muslin.
Rub it with fine-sifted sand and rushes, or wood-ash and rushes.
Rub it with the stems of horsetail.

Keep the inside of pewter pots, mugs and bowls brighter than the outside.

To clean brass and copper
Use boiling vinegar or crushed rhubarb leaves.
Crush a raw onion with damp earth and use it as a polish – it is particularly good for protecting brass from fly stains.

To clean windows
Rub them with a cut raw onion.

To clean sticky roasting tins
A solution of boiling water, soda and whitening. Wash them well with cold water after cleaning.

Breakages in the kitchen
All breakages come in threes. (This was believed so much that after breaking one piece of pottery servants and housewives would often deliberately break two more old pieces to save any of the best china being lost.)

It is lucky to break pottery on Good Friday as the points of every sherd pierce the body of Judas Iscariot.

All sorts of omens can be read into household occurrences
Alas, you know the cause too well!
The salt is spilt; to me it fell;
Then, to contribute to my loss,
My knife and fork were laid across:
On Friday, too, the day I dread!
Would I were safe at home in bed!
Last night (I vow to heaven 'tis true)
Bounce! from the fire a coffin flew.*
Next post some fatal news shall tell
God send my absent friends are well!

When hiring servants
Leave a broom on the floor when a servant comes for a job. Hire her if she picks it up.

* coffin-shaped piece of coal – once thought to be a death omen

Combating household pests

Flies

Hang a basket of different mints at the entrance to the house and touch the leaves every time you pass.
Hang a few sprigs of wormwood in every room.
Hang up or grow rue, tansy, basil and mint around the house.
Rub meat with rue leaves and the flies will not touch it.

Ants

To keep them away from the house, sprinkle the dried and powdered leaves of tansy and pennyroyal on doorsteps and window ledges.

Fleas

Fleas were known as the 'black army' and were thought to arrive on 1 March.
To be rid of them for a year, get up early on that morning, close the windows and clean every inch of the house including the doorstep and all the cracks.

While wormwood hath seed, get a handful or twaine,
To save against March to make flea to refrain:
Where chamber is sweeped, and wormwood is strowne,
No flea for his life dare abide to be known.

Pennyroyal and fennel repel fleas, and so does a decoction of rue sprinkled over the floors.

Gather as much fleabane as you can find, and each morning during June, July and August, burn a handful in every room. The smoke will drive the fleas away.

To make the house smell sweet

Burn angelica leaves every morning in a frying pan.

Burn rosemary with juniper berries to purify the air.

Hang up agrimony – its scent stays even when it is dry.

Woodruff, hung up to dry in all the rooms in summer, will keep the rooms cool and the bunches will stay fragrant for the rest of the year.

To make a pomander

Stick an orange with cloves, roll it in a mixture of ground cinnamon and orris root, rubbing them into the skin; wrap the orange in greaseproof paper and leave it in a cool, dark place for five weeks. Tie a ribbon round it and hang it up.

❀ ❀ ❀

To counteract unpleasant smells

Place a jug of milk in the room.

Put a cut onion on the shelf until it has drawn all the smell to itself – then throw it away.

Burn the roots of ploughman's spikenard.

The bedroom

To prevent nightmares, beds should always face from east to west, never north to south.

You will have bad dreams all the week if you turn the bed on Friday or Saturday.

It is unlucky to turn a feather bed on Sunday.

For sweet-smelling linen
Put the dried leaves and flowers of agrimony and woodruff amongst the sheets in the cupboard. Use them to stuff pillows and mattresses.

Other fillings for mattresses and pillows
Save wing for the feather when gander doth dye,
Save feathers of all things, the softer to lye.

To dress clean, plucked feathers for stuffing a pillow, put them in a paper bag and bake them in the oven after baking the bread.

White goose feathers are the best for pillows, but never use quill feathers as they will stick through the case and prick.

Stuff your feather bed when the moon is waning to kill the feathers completely.

Purple cotton thistle
Whereof the greatest quantitie of downe is gathered for diverse purposes, as well by the poore to stop pillowes, cushions, and beds for want of feathers as also bought of the rich Upholsterers to mix with the feathers and downe they do sell, which deceit would be looked into.

Stuff pillows and upholstery with
eel grass
oat chaff
straw
bran
cotton grass
feather top grass
reed mace from fenland reed

The weekly wash

Maides wash wel and wring wel, but beat ye wot how!

If you wash new clothes for the first time at new moon they will not wear well.

Wash your linen in the waning moon and the dirt will disappear in the dwindling light.

A liquid soap for washing clothes can be made with fat and woodash.

Old method of washing

The clothes were placed in a tub and a liquid called lye was poured through them until it ran through clean. Lye was made of a whole combination of things including soaked and drained wood ashes, hen and pigeon dung, bran water and sometimes urine which had great bleaching qualities.

Linens clean best if they are pounded with a round-ended wooden beater.

To remove stains from linen, spread it on the grass overnight in the moonlight.

Woollens can be effectively trodden in streams.

The crushed leaves of soapwort produce a lathery liquid when boiled which is excellent for washing wool.

Wash chintz in bran water.

To revitalize black silk, boil and mash ivy leaves until the water is dark and use it as a reconditioning dye.

To make a water to clean silks, soak raw potato in cold water for a day; strain the liquid and boil it.

Starch can be made from the roots of bluebells and arum lilies.

Go wash well saith Summer,
with sunne I shall dry:
Go wring well saith Winter,
with wind so shall I.

Dyeing

Plants which make dyes for cloth

warm brown – gorse

red-brown – wall lichen

dark brown – redcurrant, bracken, sorrel, walnut shells, blaeberry

dull orange – onion skins with shredded peat

yellow – camomile flowers, agrimony flowers, southernwood, dyers rocket, some types of lichen, bog myrtle (also called sweet or myrica gale, having a strong scent that repels moths), leaves and stems of cowberry, dyers greenweed (woadwax), weld (a brilliant fast dye for both cotton and wool), onion skins, apple, ash, buckthorn, birch, dog's mercury, gorse, heather, bedstraw, young alder shoots, nettle roots boiled with alum

greenish-yellow – saw-wort (woollens)

green – young heather shoots, boiled nettle leaves, lily-of-the-valley leaves with lime water, gorse, iris, broom, blackthorn, birch, elder leaves with alum

Kendal green – the cloth is first dyed yellow with dyers greenweed and then with blue woad

red – roots of green alkanet, lichen treated with tin extract, wild madder (not very bright from that grown in England – a brighter red is made from a Mediterranean species), bedstraw, tormentil, alder (woollens only)

carmine – inner bark of birch tree
magenta or purple – dandelion, elderberries, some types of lichen, oak bark
navy blue and indigo – blackberry juice
blue – buttercup root, privet (pale), blaeberry, woad, root of elecampane with ashes and whortleberries
grey – silver birch bark
black – oak, blackberry juice boiled with ivy leaves, alder bark and copperas, root and bark of elder

To dye wool
Wet the wool evenly. Bruise the ingredients for the dye and put them in the bottom of an iron pot. Cover them wit h a wooden board that has been drilled with holes. Put in the wool and pour in the water. Keep stirring the wool as the water simmers and the colour bubbles up through the holes.

Set dyes by rinsing in salt water.

To dye wool of a haire colour, first boyle your wool in alum and water and then take it forth and when it is cold take chamber lye and chimnie soote and mixing them well together boyle your wool again therein.

Care of clothes and linens
Sprinkle newly washed clothes with distilled water from the root of rose-root. They will smell very softly of roses.

Woodruff, dried and put amongst the clothes and linens, keeps away moths and makes the clothes smell like new mown hay. Brush dust from velvet with a damp goose wing.

Mending clothes
Though ladies may rend and buy new every day,
Good huswife must mend and buy new as they may.

28 August is Clothes Darning Day when all clothes must be looked over and any necessary mending done in preparation for the coming winter.

It is unlucky to mend your clothes while wearing them – you will never grow rich.

From the cradle to the grave

For centuries, birth, marriage and death have been associated with superstitious beliefs, so most of the sayings and pieces of lore regarding them seem more like fancy than fact. Some, though, contain sound pieces of advice, and many of the seemingly outrageous contain more than just a grain of truth.

Birth and upbringing: predicting births

Many nuts, few babies.

but

If there are many double nuts in the shells it will be a good year for twins.

If you rock the cradle empty
Then you shall have babies plenty.

If your apron falls from your waist a new baby is on the way.

When the event is certain

A pregnant woman should look only on beautiful things so the child will be well favoured. She must be at peace, so the baby will be contented.

Drink raspberry leaf tea throughout pregnancy for an easy birth.

Predicting the sex

Hold a length of cotton over the mother's abdomen. If it remains straight and motionless the baby will be a girl; if it moves it will be a boy.

To ease the pains of labour

Make a pain-killing cake with wholemeal flour, crushed hempseed and rhubarb root, grated dandelion root, egg yolks, milk and gin. Give slices to both the mother and the worried father.

Give the mother a caudle made of old ale, oatmeal, sugar and spices for special nourishment at the time of birth and after.

The time of birth

Most births occur when the moon is on the change.

Prosperity to the baby born at full moon.

Births are most common when the tide is coming in.

A child born on Christmas Eve, Christmas Day or Sunday is likely to be good and beautiful.

A child born on Sunday or Christmas Day will never be drowned or hanged.

A child born on Sunday has second sight.

Good Friday is the unluckiest day of the year on which to be born; but some think a Good Friday child will be gentle and possess powers of natural healing.

A child born during the chimes hours can never be bewitched and will have the power of second sight.
(What exactly the chimes hours are varies in different areas. Some say they are 8, 12 and 4 o'clock, others 3, 6, 9 and 12, and others 8, 10 and 12. Others say they are between midnight and cock-crow on Friday.)

A child born on the stroke of midnight will see spirits.

A child born between midnight and one o'clock between Friday and Saturday will be protected from witchcraft and will have the gift of natural healing.

May children and chets (kittens) never thrive.

Predicting the sex of the next child by the time of birth
If the birth occurs when the moon is waxing, the next child will be of the same sex; if when it is waning, the next child will be of the opposite sex.

Immediately after birth
Greet the baby with music, cakes and ale, and cheese.

The first journey of the child should be upwards so he will continue in that direction for the rest of his life. If he is not born downstairs, climb with him on to a stool or ladder.

Brush his face with a rabbit's foot to ward off evil spirits.

Place the new baby in the arms of a maid. It gives a boy a noble character and makes a girl modest and pure.

Wrap the baby immediately in something old like a flannel petticoat.

Roll him naked in the snow to make him strong.

The baby's first food
In different districts, the rule varies as to what this should be:
a little rue pounded with fine sugar
butter and sugar
rum butter
butter and honey
cinder water – put an ember from the fire into water and give the water to the baby. This was said to drive out the Devil.

Distinguishing marks
A child born with a cawl over his head will never be drowned as long as the cawl is preserved.

A dimple in his cheek, his living he must seek;
A dimple in his chin, his living will come in.

Moles
on the chin – success
on the thigh – misfortune
on the right temple – wealth and a high position

A strawberry mark was once taken to be the result of the mother eating too many strawberries while she was pregnant.

If a baby is born with hair on his hands and arms he will be rich.

If he has big ears the Little Folk will take care of him, as he is like one of their own.

Caring for the child
Lay a poker on the cradle to prevent a changeling being substituted.

Fairy rhyme:

When larks gin sing
Away we fling,
And babes new born steal as we go;
An elf instead we leave in bed,
And wind out laughing, Ho, ho, ho!

Hang yarrow on the cradle to make him happy and contented.

If the baby seems always hungry, give him hare's brains pounded to a jelly.

It is lucky to wean a child on Good Friday.

Never hit a naughty child with a withy stick (willow) or his growth will be stunted.

First gifts to a new baby
Put a silver coin in his hand for wealth.

Give him an egg so he will never starve, will always be clothed and always have a roof over his head.

Give him salt so he will never lack the savour of life.

True love and marriage

There's a herb in my father's garden,
  And some do call it rue;
When swallows dive and fishes fly
  Young men they shall prove true.

Whenever the cat o' the house is black
The lasses o' lovers will never ha' lack.

Who will I marry?

There are countless ways of predicting who your future spouse will be. These are just a few of the most universal:

On Midsummer's Eve place your shoes in a T and say:
Hoping this night my truelove to see,
I place my shoes in the form of a T.
(Then go to bed and dream.)

Sow hempseed in the churchyard at midnight on Midsummer's Eve in silence, and say:
These seeds I sow, swift let them grow,
Till he who must my husband be
Shall follow me and mow.
(You will see a vision of your future husband coming after you with a scythe.)

Pick an ash leaf with an even number of leaflets, put it under your pillow and say:
Even ash, even ash, I pluck thee,

This night my own true love to see.
Neither in his rick nor in his rare,
But in the clothes he everyday wear.

On St Agnes Eve (20 January) sprinkle a sprig of rosemary and one of thyme with water. Put one in each shoe and place them on either side of the bed. Then say:
St Agnes that's to lovers kind,
Ease the troubles of my mind.
(You will them dream of your future husband.)

On Hallowe'en
Prick the initials of your various suitors on crab apples, store them in the loft and do not look at them until Old Michaelmas Day (11 October). The initials of your future husband will be those that are the most perfect.

All the ladies present must hold an apple in front of the fire on a string – she whose apple falls first will marry first.

Peel an apple in one piece, hold the peel in your right hand and throw it over your left shoulder. It should fall in initial of your true love. If it breaks, you will never marry.

Also on Hallowe'en
Get some hazel nuts, give each one the name of a suitor and lay them along the edge of the fire. The one that pops the loudest and burns the brightest will bear the name of your true love.

Draw a bracken fern, cut it at the bottom of the stalk; there you will find your lover's initials.

Count every white horse till they number a hundred. The first man you shake hands with after that will be your husband whether or not he is married at the time.

A clover of two, a clover of two,
Put in your right shoe,
The first young man you meet,
In field, lane or street,
You shall have him or one of his name.

To tell if he loves you

Count the plum stones on your plate and say:
He loves me, he don't; he'll have me; he won't;
He would if he could; but he can't.

Tickle the inside of your nose with a yarrow leaf and say:
Yarroway, yarroway, bear a white blow,
If my love love me, my nose will bleed now.

When young men go courting

Carry a honeysuckle stick for luck; or a walking stick made from a branch a honeysuckle had grown round and patterned. Clinging honeysuckle represents a woman's faithful love.

To make your lover return

Stick a knife in the bladebone of a shoulder of lamb every night in a different place for nine consecutive nights, and say:
'Tis not this bonc I mean to stick,
But my true-love's heart I mean to prick,
Hoping he may not rest or sleep,
Until he comes to me to speak.

When once the Lover's Rose is dead,
Or laid aside forlorn;
Then willow-garlands, 'bout the head,
Bedew'd with tears are worne.

Test for a farmer's wife

It was the custom in one village to make the prospective wife of any local farmer lift the heavy iron lid of a chest in the church with one hand. Only if she was successful was she capable of pulling her weight on the farm and worthy of becoming his wife.

How many years until I marry?
The couple must go to a stream or pond when the moon is waxing and look at its reflection through a blue silk handkerchief. How many moons they see will be the number of years until the wedding.

Your future name
If you change the name and not the letter,
You marry for worse and not the better.

It is lucky if the initials of the bride and groom form a word.

Best time to marry
As set down by the Church
Advent marriage doth deny,
But Hilary gives the liberty;
Septuagesima says thee nay,
Eight days from Easter says you may
Rogation bids thee to contain,
But Trinity sets thee free again.

If you marry in Lent,
You will live to repent.

Marry in May,
Rue for aye.

Who marries between the sickle and the scythe,*
Will never thrive.

If you marry at full moon, prosperity will be yours.

Monday for wealth,
Tuesday for health,
Wednesday the best of all;
Thursday for losses,
Friday for crosses,
And Saturday no luck at all.

* between haymaking and harvest

Friday is a cross day for marriage.

Dean't o' Friday buy yer ring,
O' Friday dean't put spurrings* in,
Dean't wed o' Friday. Think on this
Nowther blue ner green mun match her dhriss.

The wedding dress

It is not good for a maiden to be married in colours, nor a widow in white, yet let her by all means avoid green or yellow.

Yellow is forsaken, green is forsworn.

Married in white, you have chosen alright;
Married in green, ashamed to be seen;
Married in grey, you will go far away;
Married in red, you will wish yourself dead;
Married in blue, love ever true;
Married in yellow, you're ashamed of your fellow;
Married in black, you will wish yourself back;
Married in pink, of you he'll aye think.

The bride must wear three ornaments
a ring for true love
a brooch on her breast for purity of heart
a garland on her head for joy

She must ensure happiness and felicity by carrying sprigs of rue and rosemary and a few cloves of garlic in her pocket.

On leaving the house

One last stitch must be put into the dress.

The bride must not look back.

The ring

The ring is a symbol of everlasting love, but if you have no time to buy one you can use a curtain ring or the church key.

* banns

A curtain ring wedding is a hasty wedding.

Wedding guests

Guests at country weddings used to carry bunches of green broom tied up with ribbons. Its many flowers were a symbol of good luck and prosperity.

It is lucky to have a chimney sweep at your wedding. It was thought that the bride would take one look at his dirty face and clothes and vow to keep her house clean for ever more.

Weather

Happy is the bride the sun shines on.

It is lucky to marry in a snowstorm.

Crossing the threshold

The farmer and his wife should cross the threshold together as a sign that they will work side by side.

Take weapon away, of what force is a man?
Take huswife from husband, and what is he than?

Quan the mayden hayt that che lovit,
Che is withoute longyng.
(When a maid hath that which she loves,
She longs not in her mind)

Death

Country people have always held death in great respect and its omens were many. You can perhaps imagine what it was like to experience them, but do not let them worry you. That is where our practical world has its advantage!

Death omens

a dog howling in the night three times near the house when someone was sick

bats flying three times round the house
an adder on the doorstep
seeing a butterfly at night or seeing a trio of butterflies
a swarm of bees on a dead branch
a crowing hen
the cock crowing at night
a bird perching on the windowsill or tapping at the pane
a robin on the window sill crying 'weep, weep'
a bird flying into the room
a white bird encircling the house

Hark! now everything is still,
The screech owl and the whistler shrill
Call upon the dame aloud,
And bid her quickly don her shroud.

If in your house a man shoulders a spade,
For you or your kinsfolk a grave it is made.

If you buy a broom in May,
You're sure to sweep a corpse away.

One runner bean in a row coming up white means a death in the family.

A bloom on the apple tree when apples are ripe
Is a sure termination of somebody's life.

Many nuts,
Many pits.*

For a warm wet May
The parsons do pray,
For then death-fees
Do come their way.

The moment of death

If the church clock chimes as someone is dying, it chimes sadly.

Most deaths occur during a falling tide.

A person cannot die easy on a bed of wild bird feathers.

A soul cannot pass peacefully it if lays 'athurt the planshon' (across the floorboards).

The sweepings of the floor by the altar, brought to the bedside, will shorten a lingering death.

To make the end come easy, unfasten all the boxes and locks in the house.

After death

A plate of salt placed on the corpse helped the soul on its journey.

Cover the looking-glass to prevent the soul being caught.

The passing bell was rung at country funerals to inform anyone listening whether it were a man, a woman or a child being buried. Usually it was the tenor bell and it was muffled for important persons or for a bell-ringer. Although the number of tolls varied in different places it was most often nine for a man, six for a woman and three for a child. The tolls were called knocks or tellers, hence: Nine tailors (tellers) make a man.

* graves

Hope, fear, false-joy, trouble
Are the four winds which daily toss this bubble.
His breath's a vapour and his life's a span,
'Tis glorious misery to be born a man.

God Save your soul,
Beans and all.
(Broad beans were once distributed at country funerals)

3 Nature's way

Nature's remedies

The nature of flowers, dame Physic doth show;
She teacheth them all, to be known to a few.

Every countrywoman once had a sound knowledge of the healing herbs that she acquired naturally as a child. When she or one of her brothers and sisters was ill she watched which herbs her mother went to gather. She learned where they grew, their taste and smell and how they were prepared. But so-called 'wonder drugs' changed all that. They were new, they were chemical, they were prepared in large antiseptic factories by men in white coats – they must be better – mustn't they? Nowadays, we aren't so sure: there are side effects and addictions and malformed children. Aren't the old herbs and natural diets better after all? Many people are beginning to come full circle. Herbal remedies are once more being widely used, and not just by 'cranks' but by qualified and experienced doctors.

There are enough tried and tested herbal remedies to fill several encyclopaedias. Below are just a few harmless ones for some of the more common everyday ailments. If you are really ill and don't like the drugs prescribed by conventional practitioners, do not attempt to diagnose and treat yourself. Go to a homeopath or a naturopath, and make sure first that he is qualified.

Many of the old remedies were made with herbs and flowers that are now rare, so I have excluded them. The plants need to be protected as well as ourselves.

One or two of the more outlandish cures have been included just for amusement and others because they could easily have worked by suggestion, rather like placebo pills. Recently, there was a vogue for hanging a small chain from the back of the car to prevent travel sickness. No one knew quite why it worked. Probably the feeling of the sufferer was: 'The chain is there so I will be alright' – and he was. Should we laugh, then, at someone tying periwinkle stems round his leg to prevent cramp?

An ideal situation in medicine would be if the natural remedies could be tested by modern science and proven true or false. Those that worked, we could use and improve on by discovering the best proportions and amounts to be effective. This is the basis of homeopathic medicine and it should be the basis of all medicine.

Nature has given us many gifts and the countryman has known them for centuries.

Sage, hibiscus and marigold,
Excellent herbs had our fathers of old.

Colds and coughs

The common cold is probably the most prevalent of minor ailments, so perhaps it deserves a little more space than the rest. There is still no cure for it once it has developed, but if you heed the warning signs your body puts out to you it is often possible to prevent it from taking hold. If you start to sneeze for no apparent reason, feel slightly tired and cold from the inside out, then a cold is probably waiting to pounce. Don't let it. The best cold-stopper is blackberry cordial. If you make about four bottles every year they will keep you going until the next blackberry season.

When you suspect a lurking cold put 1.5 dl (¼ pint) of blackberry cordial into a 3 dl (½ pint) mug and top it up with boiling water. Retire to bed early and drink the cordial in bed, as hot as you can, and go to sleep. You may find you sweat a bit in the night but by the next morning you should feel better. If not, do the same the following night.

Blackberry cordial

Put 4.5 litres (1 gallon) of blackberries into a preserving pan with 6 tablespoons water. Tie 1 tablespoon each allspice berries

and cloves, a piece of cinnamon stick and several nutmeg chips in a muslin bag and add these to the blackberries. Cook very gently until the blackberries are soft and pulpy and the pan is full of juice. Strain them through muslin and measure the juice. Return it to the pan with 300 g (10 oz) of honey to each litre. Stir on a low heat until the honey has dissolved and then simmer for 10 minutes. Take the pan from the heat and stir in a quarter bottle of brandy. Cool the cordial, bottle and cork it. Store it in a cool dark place.

Elderberry rob
This is as good as the blackberry cordial and can be made in exactly the same way but with 3 dl (½ pint) of water for the first simmering.

Rosehip syrup
If you can't find any blackberries or elderberries, pick rosehips after the second frost and make rosehip syrup, using honey instead of sugar and cutting the amount by one-third. This, too, is an excellent cold preventer.

What do you drink during the day when you feel a cold coming on? Coffee and tea will only make you feel worse. Herb teas are soothing and comforting, and some of them will carry on the fight that the cordial started the night before.

Mint and yarrow tea always feels very soothing as you drink it. Infuse a teaspoon of each in 3 dl (½ pint) of boiling water and sweeten it with a teaspoon of honey.

Onions and garlic help to allay cold symptoms. A hot bowl of cheese and onion soup makes a good late night supper, with a fresh salad dressed with lemon juice and lots of crushed garlic.

If you can bear it, hold a peeled clove of garlic between your cheek and teeth on both sides for some time during the day.

Or drink hot milk with crushed garlic in it.

Don't drink too much alcohol when you have a cold – it burns up the Vitamin C.

Sore throats often go hand in hand with colds. Gargling will soothe them. Use walnut husks boiled with honey, or an infusion of elderflowers.

Also for sore throats, an infusion* of sage leaves and honey. Infuse 30 sage leaves in 6 dl (1 pint) of boiling water for 30 minutes. Add 2 tablespoons cider vinegar and 2 tablespoons honey. Take a teaspoon whenever necessary or use it as a gargle several times a day.

* An infusion is made like tea. Boiling water is poured on the fresh or dried herb.
A decoction is made by boiling the herb in a large amount of water, so the liquid reduces and all the goodness is extracted from the leaves or roots or whatever part of the plant you are using.

If the cold runs its course and leaves a cough behind, coltsfoot is one of the most effective remedies. It was once made into a candy but is just as good as a tea. Make a decoction by putting 25 g (1 oz) of leaves into 1 litre (2 pints) of water and boiling until you are left with 6 dl (1 pint). Strain the liquid, sweeten it with honey and drink a teacupful at intervals during the day.

Hyssop tea soothes a hacking cough. Infuse 1 tablespoon in 6 dl (1 pint) of boiling water and sweeten it with honey.

Drink an infusion of 1 teaspoon lungwort leaves in 1 cup of boiling water several times a day.

Drink a decoction of the root of feverfew.

Take a small spoonful of the decoction of the root of elecampane three times a day; or infuse the roots with honey in white wine; or make a candy by steeping the roots in syrup.

Red cabbage syrup eases coughs. Pound the leaves and squeeze out the juice. Boil it to a syrup with half its weight in honey.

Spread goose grease on brown paper and wear it on your chest, or make a hot poultice of goose grease. (I have an uncle who swears by it.) Make sure you wear a thick vest and an old shirt!

Sneezing

I could only find one remedy for sneezing – dose the body with a hearty drink of wine or other strong liquor till it is thoroughly heated!

Whooping cough
The exceptional number of country remedies that exist for whooping cough suggest that it was once one of the commonest of diseases. Whichever remedy you tried, it was said that the disease should always go in May but if it didn't it would stay all summer.

There are herbal remedies and innumerable charms and rituals which were probably last-resort measures for a disease that was particularly difficult to cure.

A donkey often featured in some way. The suffering child was passed over and under the animal for a set number of times, or he may have been given a remedy containing a set number of hairs from the donkey's back.

The patient was passed through a bramble arch nine times while a charm was repeated; and as a preventative a briar cross was worn round the neck.

A spider or hairy caterpillar was tied in a bag round the child's neck and as it died the disease went with it.

Bread and butter given by a couple called John and Joan, or Joseph and Mary was another cure.

The last resort was to ask any man on a piebald (or sometimes skewbald) horse. His answer was usually 'buttered ale'.

Mice, either fried, roasted, cooked with onions or dried were a countrywide remedy.

It was thought good for the sufferer if he could be taken out in the early morning to inhale sheeps' breath, or into the cattle shed to breathe in the sweet breath of the cows.

The following herbal remedies help to allay the symptoms of whooping cough and eventually bring on a cure.
Infuse 25 g (1 oz) dried thyme in 6 dl (1 pint) boiling water, sweeten with honey and have 1 tablespoon four times a day.

Infuse 25 g (1 oz) dried mouse-ear hawkweed in 6 dl (1 pint) boiling water, sweeten with honey and take a wineglassfull three times a day.

Do the same with dried red clover.

Drink an infusion of dried honeysuckle flowers several times a day.

Infuse 50 g (2 oz) of the fresh flowering tips of marjoram in 9 dl ($1\frac{1}{2}$ pints) boiling water for 10 minutes. Take three cupfuls a day, each one before a meal.

Boil 8 cabbage leaves in 1 litre (2 pints) water for 30 minutes. Strain and sweeten with honey. Take a cupful four times a day.

Simmer a lettuce in 6 dl (1 pint) water for 20 minutes. Drink three cupfuls of the liquid a day between meals.

Pour 6 dl (1 pint) boiling water on to 225 g (8 oz) crushed or chopped garlic, leave it for 12 hours and sweeten with honey. Take 1 teaspoonful every 2 hours.

Roast some sunflower seeds in the oven, crush them and use them to make an infusion.

Influenza

There are very few old remedies for 'flu' so it must be more of a modern complaint.

Elderberries are the best medicine for flu.
Drink hot elderberry wine.

Make a strong infusion of elderberries and peppermint. Let it steep for 30 minutes and drink it just before settling down to sleep.

Boil 25 g (1 oz) borage in 9 dl (1½ pints) water for 3 minutes and leave them to infuse for 15 minutes. Drink a cupful four or five times a day.

Make agrimony tea with 25 g (1 oz) dried agrimony infused in 6 dl (1 pint) boiling water. Drink it several times a day.

Infuse 6 g (¼ oz) dried hyssop in 6 dl (1 pint) boiling water for 10 minutes. Sweeten it with honey and drink a cupful three times a day.

Headaches

Headaches are usually brought about by tension and worry, and many of the herbal remedies have a calming and relaxing effect.

Camomile tea is a great calmer. Make it in a covered jug or teapot: use 25 g (1 oz) dried camomile to 6 dl (1 pint) boiling water and let it infuse for 10 minutes. (This tea, made with barley water and sweetened with honey is also good for fretting or hyperactive children.)

Ground ivy, betony, feverfew and rosemary teas soothe nervous headaches. Use 25 g (1 oz) of each herb, dried, to 6dl (1 pint) boiling water and sweeten to taste with honey. Cool and take a wineglassful four times a day. (Make up each herb separately.)

If your headache is brought about by overwork, drink a weak infusion of lavender flowers.

Wear lavender flowers under your hat to ease headache or dab lavender water on the brow and temples.

To make lavender water

Steep 2 tablespoons dried lavender flowers, 1 tablespoon sweet cicely leaves, 2 teaspoon dried cinnamon and 1 grated nutmeg in

1 litre (2 pints) surgical spirits for 2 weeks. Strain, bottle and seal tightly.

Lie down, lay fresh rue leaves on your temples and gently chew one or two of them in an easy, relaxed way.

To cool a spinning head, lay down and cover your forehead with cucumber peel.

Insomnia

Sit down and relax before going to bed. Eat an apple and drink a glass of country wine or vintage cider; or a mug of hot milk and honey.

Milk and honey is also good in the small hours when you feel you are never going to sleep again. It warms and soothes from the inside out.

Other bedtime drinks

Put 25 g (1 oz) chopped peppermint, 12 g (½ oz) rue and 12 g (½ oz) wood betony in a teacup. Pour on boiling water, stir, cover and leave for 20 minutes. Strain and sweeten with honey.

Balm tea

Infuse 25 g (1 oz) dried leaves in 9 dl (1½ pints) boiling water and sweeten with honey.

Use a hop pillow; or a pillow of herbs including lady's mantle and agrimony:

If it (agrimony) be leyd under mann's heed
He shal sleepyn as he were deed;
He shal never drede ne wakyn
Till fro under his heed it be takyn.

If you have a nightmare, calm yourself down with camomile tea.

Indigestion

Garlic is a good preventative. If the meal hasn't included it, infuse 1 crushed or chopped clove in 3 dl (½ pint) boiling water and drink a cupful afterwards.

Chew the dried root of sweet sedge (calamus); or infuse 25 g (1 oz) of the dried root in 6 dl (1 pint) boiling water. Drink it, when you need it, by the teacupful.

Take 25 g (1 oz) dried root of carline thistle gathered in the autumn. Boil it in 9 dl (1½ pints) water for 5 minutes and let it infuse for 10 minutes. Drink three cupfuls a day between meals.

Infuse 25 g (1 oz) dried centaury in 6 dl (1 pint) boiling water and take a wineglassful half an hour before meals. If you find it bitter, add a little mint or angelica. (This is also good if you are suffering from loss of appetite.)

Hiccoughs

Hiccoughs can appear for no apparent reason at the most embarrassing times.

If you are away from home, hold your breath and swallow the 'hic' or try to sneak a glass of water into the bathroom and drink out of it backwards.

At home, one of the best remedies is to drink 1 teaspoon mustard powder dissolved in a teacup of hot water. Do it again 10 minutes later if they still haven't gone.

Spearmint and wood betony tea (each made with 25 g (1 oz) to 6 dl (1 pint) water) are also good.

Inhale the fumes of dill seeds boiled in wine. (This is an old one, not tested.)

Try and say this rhyme, drinking a glass of water:

Hiccups, hiccups,
Rise up Jacob,
Seven gullups in the cup
Cure hiccups.

Upset stomach
Eat plain, fairly filling foods such as wholemeal bread (with no butter), a jacket-baked potato, or porridge made with water and sweetened with a very little honey.

Drink dandelion tea sweetened with honey.

Drink an infusion of dried elderberries.

Make a settling medicine by boiling 12 g (½ oz) of the dried root of herb bennet (avens) in 6 dl (1 pint) water until the liquid is reduced by half. Strain and cool it before drinking. (At one time it was stipulated that the root had to be dug up from dry ground on 25 March.)

Another medicine
25 g (1 oz) of the powdered root of tormentil infused in 6 dl (1 pint) boiling water.

Put a sliced onion on a tin plate in the bedroom of the sufferer overnight. It acts as a disinfectant, drawing all the germs to it. Burn it in the morning.

Cramp
Drink a warm infusion of pennyroyal.

Tie periwinkle stems round the leg or arm that is most likely to be affected.

Wear the patella of a sheep.

Put corks under your pillow to stop cramp occurring in the middle of the night.

If cramp is really bad, it does help to shout something. This is an old charm:
The cramp is keenless,
Mary was sinless
When she bore Jesus.
Let the cramp go away,
In the name of Jesus.

Rheumatism

Rheumatism was once a common country complaint and there were almost as many remedies for it as there were for whooping cough, although mostly they were rather more practical.

Nowadays, sufferers wear copper bangles, and carrying or wearing some special object has long been thought of as a preventative.

A potato was perhaps the most common. It had to be placed in your clothes, unseen by a member of the opposite sex. Then you had to carry it everywhere you went, transferring it yourself from garment to garment. The smaller and harder it became, the less likely were you to suffer from rheumatism.

Apples in any form help to cure rheumatism
Lay a poultice of rotten apples on the aching limb.
Drink a glass of dry cider every day.
Have a teaspoon of cider vinegar every morning before breakfast

Rub the aching limb with oil of mustard.

Dip a cloth in a hot infusion of tansy and wrap it round the leg or arm that aches.

Make a poultice of grated horseradish soaked in boiling milk.

Drink an infusion of marigold flowers three or four times a day.

Boil 25 g (1 oz) dandelion root in 9 dl (1½ pints) water for 20 minutes, strain and drink half a cupful twice a day.

Infuse 1 teaspoon celery seeds in 1 cup boiling water and drink this three times a day.

Eat celery cooked in milk.

Garters were worn as a preventative measure
In the summer, make garters of dried and softened eel skins and stuff them with lavender; bury them in peat between layers of mint and they will be ready in the autumn. The garters can be worn by both sexes, just above the knee, on the right leg for men and on the left for women.

Sciatica
Boil nettles in water, strain them and use the water for a hot poultice.

Lay bruised rue leaves on the aching part.

Neuralgia
Apply a poultice of vervain.

Crush equal parts of camomile flowers and poppyheads to make a poultice.

Drink an infusion of feverfew.

Toothache
Old ways of preventing toothache
Bite the first fern of the year.
Carry a double hazelnut.
Carry a rabbit's tooth or a hedgehog's skull.
Chew on an elder twig or have a toothpick made of elder wood.

To ease the pain
Put a few drops oil of cloves or oil of marjoram on a piece of cotton wool and place it in the hollow of the aching tooth.

Do the same with onion juice.

Soften the flowers of common mallow in hot water and chew on them.

Rest your face on a pillow of warm hops.

This charm, written on a piece of paper and hung round your neck in a bag, was once a preventative:
As Peter sat weeping on a marvel stone, Christ came by and said unto him, 'Peter, what ailest thou?' Peter answered and said unto him, 'My Lord and my God, my tooth acheth.' Jesus said unto him, 'Arise, Peter, and be thou whole; and not thou only but all them that carry these lines for my sake shall never have toothache.'

Earache
Hold any of these to your ear
a cotton bag of camomile heads that has been warmed by the fire
a hot, roasted onion
a pad of cotton wool soaked in warm parsley juice.

There are many country remedies for minor ailments brought about through working outside in all weathers.

Chapped lips and noses
Rub them with goose grease.

Chapped hands
Massage them with a strong decoction of spearmint.

Bind them round with the udder wool of a ewe to make a natural lanoline dressing.

Rub them with broom salve
Put some clarified lard in a large basin or crock and melt it down. Put in as much broom or gorse blossom as you can possibly mix in and leave overnight in the warm. Melt the lard again if necessary and strain, pressing down on the blossoms. Keep doing this until the lard becomes yellow. Pour it into little pots and cover.

Thorns and splinters
Bathe them with an infusion of hawthorn leaves.

Nettle stings
Rub them with a dock leaf – it never fails to work even if the stings are severe.

This charm was once repeated at the same time. As with cramp, shouting something does help to take your mind off the pain:

Nettle out, dock in,
Dock remove nettle sting,
In dock, out nettle,
Don't let the blood settle.

Bee and wasp stings

Dab them with vinegar.

Rub them with a cut leek or onion.

Apply the leaves of common mallow crushed with olive oil.

Rub them with crushed plantain leaves or crushed marigold flowers.

Rub them with bruised thyme leaves.

Other insect bites

Rub them with the cut stem of houseleek.

Dab salt on them.

Bathe them with an infusion of feverfew. (This also helps to keep them away, so if you are going to work outside bathe your hands and arms before you start.)

Bruises

Ease the pain by rubbing them with an onion.

Rub them with chopped marjoram pounded with honey, or with oil of marjoram.

Bathe them with an infusion of hyssop leaves.

Make a poultice of the fresh roots of Solomon's Seal.

Make a decoction of nettle flowers, strain it and bathe the bruise with the liquid.

If the bruise is swollen, beat bruised nettles, salt and vinegar into lard and apply as an ointment.

For a black eye, tie hyssop leaves in a linen cloth and soak them in boiling water; cool them slightly and hold them over the eye.

Cuts and grazes

Bathe them with a infusion of marigold flowers – it will ease pain and bleeding and to a certain extent lessen scarring.

Apply a poultice of pounded root or leaves of comfrey; or bathe with an infusion of comfrey leaves.

To stop bleeding, bind round bandages dipped in a decoction of the leaves or powdered dried root of lady's mantle; or make a poultice of the bruised leaves of common plantain.

Ointment for cuts and grazes

Put fresh elderflowers in an equal amount of lard, heat them gently until the flowers are crisp and strain the lard through linen, pressing down hard on the flowers.
A similar ointment can be made with lard and the leaves of white horehound.

If you are cut with a knife or any metal object whatever, it must be cleaned and polished at the same time as the wound is cleaned and dressed, otherwise the wound will go septic. (Old country belief)

Burns and scalds

Bathe them with an infusion of houseleek; or of houseleek and common plantain together.

Apply the bruised fresh leaves of houseleek or common plantain in the form of a poultice.

Bruised comfrey leaves applied as a poultice will take away the sting.

Bathe with a decoction of mullein, made by boiling 50 g (2 oz) of the leaves in 9 dl (1½ pints) water for 5 minutes.

Sprains

Make a soothing ointment by warming 3 parts elder leaves to 4 parts lard and 2 parts grated suet. When the lard has turned green, strain it through linen. Cool, and store in airtight pots.

Or, take 225 g (8 oz) elder leaves, 100 g (4 oz) leaves of common plantain, 50 g (2 oz) ground ivy and 100 g (4 oz) wormwood (all fresh). Chop them and mix them into 2 kg (4 lb) melted lard. Put them in a crock in a low oven until the leaves are crisp. Strain the lard through linen.

Also for sprains, make a poultice of fresh tansy leaves.

Chilblains

As long as chilblains are unbroken, you can treat them yourself and ease the pain and sometimes cure them completely.

To prevent them

Wear open, thick-soled sandals around the house in winter so your feet can breathe.

Don't wear plastic or rubber shoes indoors in cold weather.

Bathe your feet regularly with a decoction of marigold flowers and sea salt.

To ease the pain

Rub them with salt and onion; or apply a poultice of a little grated onion and salt.

Soak your feet in a bath to which you have added a little lemon juice.

Make a poultice of grated raw potato and salt.

Apply the pounded roots of black bryony.

Steep the berries and roots of black bryony in gin and use it as a lotion.

Rub them with a tallow candle.

Bathe them in a decoction of oak bark.

Make a poultice of boiled marigold leaves.

If you dip a newborn baby's feet in snow, he will never have chilblains.

Corns

As a preventative

Run barefoot as often as possible in the early morning dew.

When you have them

Bind on ivy leaves and vinegar.

Bind on a pad of unwashed sheep's wool.

Rub the corns every day with a cut clove of garlic.

Soak chopped leeks in water for twenty-four hours and apply them to the corn several nights running. This makes them easy to remove.

Cut corns in the waning moon and they will gradually disappear.

Warts

You rarely get badly troubled with warts these days but there were once so many ways of charming them away that it seems that there must have been a lot of warty people around. All over the country, they were tying knots in string, sticking snails with thorns, stealing steak, cutting notches in twigs and burying things at dead of night. A basic method was to rub the warts with something that would rot, bury whatever it was, and as it decayed the warts would disappear. Who can tell whether it worked or not? I do know, though, that you really can wish them away on the new moon. I know someone who has done it several times. As long as you believe it will work, it does.

If you can't muster up that kind of faith, try these

Dab on the juice of houseleek.

Slice the thick leaves of houseleek in two and bind them on to the wart, cut side down.

Apply green willow rind soaked in vinegar.

Pound chopped lesser celandine with lard and use it as an ointment.

Apply the juice of the pounded leaves of common meadow buttercup.

Make a strong decoction of the bruised root of tormentil by boiling 50 g (2 oz) in 1 litre (2 pints) water so the liquid reduces by one third. Soak a piece of lint in it and dab it on the warts.

Rub the wart with the furry inside of a broad bean pod.

To ensure good health
To eat an apple going to bed,
Makes the doctor beg his bread.

If they would drink nettles in March
And eat mugwort in May,
So many fine maidens
Wouldn't go to clay.

Eat leeks in lide (March)
And ramsins in May,
And all the year after
Physicians may play.

If you'd live to be old,
Strip before you sweat
And dress before you're cold.

Natural beauty

Pride must abide.

There are two ways to beauty: making sure that your face and hair stay in good condition; and camouflaging with cosmetics and dyes when you haven't taken the right care. Country women have little time to stand in front of the mirror every morning,

and wind and weather play havoc with daintily set hair and eye make-up, so natural beauty and skin care must be the choice.

Hair care

One of the most beneficial herbs for the hair is rosemary, especially if your hair goes from mid-brown to dark. It stimulates the hair bulbs and regular use can prevent early balding.

The most simple way of using rosemary is to make an infusion, cool it and use it as a rinse after washing your hair.

If you have dry hair, infuse 25 g (1 oz) rosemary in 6 dl (1 pint) olive oil, and leave it standing for a week on a sunny window sill. Massage it into your scalp and wrap your hair up in a hot towel for 10 minutes before you wash it.

If your hair is greying or you simply want to darken it a little, make a strong infusion of sage and rosemary and use it as a rinse.

Rosemary hair-wash to keep hair healthy and prevent dandruff
Infuse 25 g (1 oz) dried rosemary and 2 teaspoons borax in 6 dl (1 pint) boiling water; let it cool and use it like shampoo.

Camomile flowers are good for blonde hair. Infuse 25 g (1 oz) dried flowers in 6 dl (1 pint) boiling water; cool and strain and use as a rinse.

For soft, glossy hair, simmer 225 g (8 oz) young nettles in 1 litre (2 pints) water for 2 hours. Strain and bottle and use as a rinse. To prevent baldness, rub the infusion well into the scalp every other night.

For dandruff, put 1 teaspoon cider vinegar into a glass of water and comb it through the hair morning and evening.

If you cut your hair at the time of the new moon it will grow thick as the moon waxes.

For the complexion
Bean pods steeped in wine and vinegar, and bean meal mixed with milk were once commonly used to make the complexion smooth and soft.

A sun-tanned face was once thought to be unattractive, and many herbal infusions were applied to try and lessen the sun's effects. Nowadays, a brown, healthy-looking face is coveted by most women, but if you sit in the sun too long, your skin can become over dry. Then the old lotions can be beneficial.

To refresh after sunbathing and after swimming in salt water
Press elderflowers into a large jar and fill it up with boiling water. Add 3 dl (1½ fl oz) rectified spirits, cover with a tea cloth and stand in a warm place for 2 hours. Cool, strain, bottle and cork. Dab it on your face or put a little in the bath.

Hang elderflowers in the bath in a muslin bag to cool sunburnt skin.

Wild strawberries beautify the skin and help sunburn. Rub a cu wild strawberry over your face immediately after washing, or if the face is badly sunburnt, make a face-pack of crushed wild strawberries.

Lighten freckles with an infusion of dandelion flowers. Boil a handful of the flowers in 9 dl (1½ pints) water for 30 minutes. Cool it and wash the face with it morning and evening. You can also do the same with a bunch of parsley.

Refreshing nettle face pack
Put 450 g (1 lb) chopped young nettle leaves into a saucepan with about 1 cm (½ in) water, cover them and set them on a low heat for 15 minutes. Spread them on thin muslin and lay it on your face for 15 minutes. Wash the nettles off with warm water and lemon juice.

A face pack of pulped apples will make the skin firm and help keep away wrinkles.

To remove blotches and combat wrinkles mix grated raw carrot and lemon juice. Lay them over your face and leave for 30 minutes.

And it's dabbling in the dew makes the milkmaids fair.
Early morning dew is beautifying for the complexion. At one time it had to be gathered from specific plants such as lady's mantle, but May dew was considered the best of all:
The fair maid who the first of May,
Goes to the field at break of day,
And washes in dew from the hawthorn tree,
Will ever after handsome be.

❀ ❀ ❀

Hands
Whiten them by rubbing them with lemon juice or the lemon rinds left after squeezing the juice for cooking.

Massage honey and lemon into housework hands to make them soft and white.

Boil some floury potatoes and mash them with milk. Rub them into your hands every evening.

Teeth

Fresh sage leaves rubbed on the teeth will cleanse and strengthen the gums.

To whiten teeth, rub them with pulped wild strawberries, leave them for 5 minutes and rinse with warm water to which you have added a very little bicarbonate of soda.

Tobacco

Herbal tobacco

The main ingredient of herbal tobacco should be coltsfoot. To it you can add woodruff, comfrey leaves, red clover flowers, camomile flowers, and a few chestnut and beech leaves.

To make coltsfoot tobacco

Gather coltsfoot after the flowers have died.
Hang the whole plants up to dry.
Tear away the stems and pack the leaves in a wooden box.
Lace them with a little brandy and keep them on the mantelpiece.

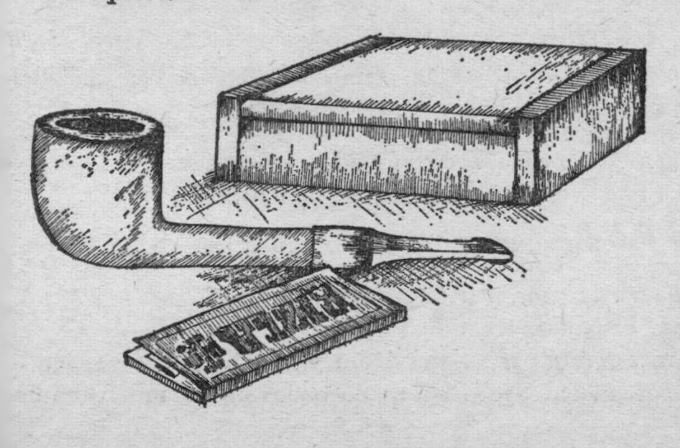

To cure and grow tobacco plants

Tobacco seed looks like fine dust.

Set it in trays in the greenhouse and plant out the young seedlings in June.

Light, sandy soils are best for tobacco.

Dress the plants every month with saltpetre – two or three pinches for each plant. Scatter it well round the roots.

Pinch out all the flower buds and lateral growths so the leaves grow nice and big, but don't start pruning until the colour of th first flowers appears.

Tobacco plants are ready for harvesting when the leaves crack when they are folded across. Ripe leaves droop slightly and snap off easily when they are twisted sideways.

Start harvesting in late August and pick off the separate leaves as they mature.

Harvest only in dry weather, preferably at midday.

Split the base of the stems and thread a thin cane or a piece of wire through all the leaves so you can hang them up to dry. You should get fifty leaves on a 1-m (3-ft) length.

Hang the leaves in a warm, dry, airy shed.

Tobacco leaves are like a weather glass – when the weather is damp so are they.

When the leaves are dry (about the end of November) take them down and pack them fairly loosely in cardboard boxes.

Put them under the spare-room bed and leave them for a year o more. (The longer they are left, the better the final result.)

Every season produces a different coloured leaf.

To cure the tobacco you will need

a square biscuit tin

a mixture of four parts water to one part either black treacle, molasses, golden syrup, honey, Barbados sugar, rum, fruit juic

Tear the midribs from the leaves (You can grind them to make snuff or boil them to make insecticide.)

The leaves from the middle of the plant will produce the best tobacco and those from the bottom will be rather coarse. You can either separate or mix them.

Watch your hands – they will be stained yellow.

Pack the leaves in layers in your biscuit tin, sprinkling each layer with the flavouring mixture.

Put the lid on and put the tin into the oven which has been heated to 180°C (350°F) Gas No. 4. Leave it for 2 hours, turning it over halfway through the cooking time so the juices have a chance to run through the leaves again.

Take off the lid, turn off the oven and let the leaves cool where they are.

Take out the leaves and crumble them in your fingers. This makes a fairly dry tobacco that smells like Havana cigars.

To make a block of moist smoking mixture
Cure the leaves with the spines intact.
Wrap the cured leaves in damp cotton, leave them for a day and then tear out the spines.
Set a small wooden box with a weight that fits the top exactly.
Lay single layers of tobacco leaves in the box and brush them with the same flavouring mixture that you used for curing. Pack them tight and press them for twenty-four hours. Take out the block and shred it up.
Don't press too much at once as if you don't smoke it fast enough it will mildew.
It takes a little experience to get the mixture right, as if it's too damp it won't burn and if it's too dry it will burn your mouth.
Smoke the tobacco in a pipe or made into cigarettes or cigars.

You may take a pipe if you please,
Likewise a chair to sit as ease.

The country garden

Through cunning, with dibble, rake, mattock and spade,
By line and by level, trim garden is made.

Most gardening lore comes from the country where it is second nature to those who have been born and bred there; but it can also be applied to every window box and tiny piece of cultivated land in towns or cities.

Vitality flows through the soil, so it must be healthy and not drug-addicted.

Expensive chemicals are detrimental to the soil, the plants and the environment.

Soil needs humus, nourishment and trace elements.

Plants cannot take up minerals without humus in the soil.

A good soil shouldn't stick to your boots, even when it's wet.

The compost heap

Don't put earthy roots on the compost heap: the earth will lower the temperature and the roots of Brussels sprouts and greens especially may cause fungus problems.

Nettles make a good addition to the compost.

Horseradish leaves are good for compost as the plant has long roots which draw up large quantities of minerals.

Other ways of enriching the soil

Comfrey has deep roots which draw up potash and phosphates, so lay the leaves on the soil for compost, particularly between rows of potatoes and round the tomato plants in the greenhouse.

Burn straw on top of the soil in August to enrich it with potash.

To make a liquid manure, soak a sack of compost in 18 litres (4 gallons) of water.

Put the first clippings of your lawn into your bean trenches with mushroom compost and newspaper.

Grow vetches or lucern and dig them in for green manure.

Keep the ground covered with weeds in the winter and the worms will turn the soil for you underneath.

Clearing the land

Clear the weeds from the surface of the soil in spring with a longhorn hoe.

If horseradish has spread too far, don't dig it up or it will spread even more. Hoe it instead.

Keep dandelions and chickweed round the edge of the garden and use them for salads.

Nettles make soup, herbal remedies and excellent compost, so keep as many as you can.

Weeds

Don't pull them in May,
Wait till another day.

Thistles cut in May
Come up again next day.

Thistles cut in June,
Come up again soon.
Thistles cut in July,
They'll be sure to die.

Cut your thistles before St John (24 June)
You will have two instead of one.

Oft digging, removing and weeding (ye see),
Make herbe the more wholesome and greater to be.

Vegetables

The sayings relating to vegetable planting apply just as much to the farmer as they do to the small-scale gardener, and many of them were used in such a context when they were first written down.

Farmers realized that there was a connection between the phases of the moon and the way their crops grew. When chemical fertilizers took over from natural organic ones these influences were forgotten:

Artificial fertilizers make the soil deaf to the music of the spheres.

Now there is an increasing number of farmers who work their land biodynamically (work in conjunction with the moon and other planets). They realize that this is not the farming of the past but of the future, as oil-based fertilizers will not last for much longer.

There are five moon rhythms that it is possible to work with: The old sayings refer only to the new moon/full moon cycle. They are very basic, but they are worth paying heed to for the beginnings of understanding are there:

Pay heed to the moon as it is the very moment that you put the seed into the earth that matters.

The moon is a gateway for effects to come into the sphere of life.

Time faire, to set or to gather be bold,
But set or remove when the weather is cold.
Cut all things or gather, the moon in the wane,
but sowe in increasing, or give it his bane.

Seeds of above-ground plants should be sown at new moon so the waxing moon draws them up.

Watery plants (marrows, cucumbers) are best set at full moon.

Set root crops when the moon is dark or during the waning moon.

Set peas and beans at the wane of the moon, and onions, carrots and parsnips at the change.

Set onion seed on the fourth new moon of the year.

Set garlicks and beanes at St Edmund the King, (20 November),
The moon in the wane, thereon hangeth a thing.

Sow peason and beanes in the wane of the Moone,
Who soweth them sooner, he soweth too soone.
That they with the planet may rest and arise,
And flourish with bearing, most plentifulwise.

February waan (wane),
Sow peas and baan (beans).

(Peas and beans grow differently to other top vegetables, and they take in a lot of nitrogen.)

Cucumbers, radishes, turnips, leeks, lilies, horseradish and saffron all increase during the full moon.

Onions are much larger and better nourished during the wane.

Sowing and setting

Sow dry and set wet.

Sow seeds in the afternoon when the earth is drawing in.

It is better to raise seeds indoors first than to set them directly outside.

Aim for short, sturdy roots on your seedlings and only plant out those that are the most vigorous.

Don't water newly set plants too late in the day – they don't like to be shivering in their shoes.

At spring (for the somer) sowe garden ye shall,
At harvest (for winter) or sowe not at all.

And set (as a daintie) thy runcivall pease. (January).

On Candlemas Day if the thorns hang adrop,
Then you are sure of a good pea crop. (2 February)

At Candlemas Day
Sow beans in the clay.
Sow beans in the mud
And they'll grow like wood.

Graie peason or runcivals cheerely to stand,
At Candlemas sowe, with a plentiful hand.

On St Valentine's Day
Beans should be in the clay.

Sow peas and beans on David and Chad,
Be the weather good or bad. (1 and 2 March)

In March and in April, from morning to night,
In sowing and setting, good huswives delight:
To have in a garden, or other like plot,
To turn up their house, and furnish their plot.

Sow onions on St Gregory (12 March) for a good crop.

If you want a parsnip good and sweet,
Sow it when you sow your wheat. (March)

When elum leaves are as big as a farden,*
It's time to plant kidney beans in the garden.

The sixth of May
Is kidney bean day. (Others say 1, 5 or 8 May.)

Who pescods would gather, to have with the last,
To serve for his household til harvest be past,
Must sowe them in Maie, in a corner ye shall,
Where through so late growth no hindrance may fall.

Be it weal or be it woe,
Beans should blow† before May go.

Green peason or hastings at Hallontide sow,
In hartie good soile he requireth to growe. (11 November.)

To do well, shallots must be sown on the shortest day of the year, and pulled on the longest.

Broad beans must be sown on St Thomas's Day. (21 December)

Potatoes

Potato seed should never be bought from a place south of you.

Use long-shooted seed potatoes to increase your yield.

Plant potatoes with a rising tide so they grow with it.

Sow potatoes when the yellow wagtail arrives in spring.

March is the best season of the year for planting potatoes.

Plant your taturs when you will,
They won't come up before April.

Old Man Dumbledead
Tilled his garden full of seed,
When the seed beginned to grow
Like a garden full of snow,
When the snow beginned to melt

* farthing
† flower

Like a garden full of silk,
When the silk beginned to fly
Like an eagle in the sky,
When the sky beginned to roar
Like a lion at my door,
When my door beginned to creak
Like a stick put 'bout my back,
When my back beginned to smart
Like a penknife through my heart,
When my heart begins to bleed,
That's the time for sowing seed.

Herbs

Although cottage gardens have always blossomed with flowers there were very few plants that could be described as 'not being used either in meate nor medicine, but esteemed for their beautie to deck up gardens and bosomes of the beautiful'. All the flowers had a purpose and mostly came under the heading of 'herbs'.

Even in tiny gardens, you can have a small plot for cooking herbs and, if there is room, for medicinal herbs and those for herb teas. For a garden border you can have sweet smelling lavender and other aromatic plants. Here are just a few to choos from.

Herbs for the pot

Alecost (garden tansy)
Basil
Bay
Burnet
Caraway
Chervil
Chives
Coriander
Dill
Fennel
Good King Henry
Lovage
Marigold
Marjoram
Mint (several kinds)
Parsley
Rosemary
Sage
Savory (summer and winter)
Sorrel
Tarragon
Thyme and Lemon Thyme
Welsh Onion

Herbs for teas and drinks

Agrimony
Lemon Balm
Borage (for summer fruit cups)
Camomile
Meadowsweet
Melilot
Peppermint

Medicinal herbs

Alkanet
Greater celandine
Coltsfoot
Comfrey
Feverfew
Horehound (black and white)
Houseleek
Meadowsweet
Mullein
St John's wort
Wild strawberry
Tansy
Valerian
Vervain
Yarrow

Aromatic herbs

Artemisias (wormwood, southernwood, lady's mantle)
Balm of Gilead
Bergamots (scarlet, purple, rose)
Catmints
Clary sage
Cotton lavenders
Elecampane
Geraniums
Heliotrope
Hyssop
Jerusalem sage
Lavenders
Lemon verbena
Mints
Pennyroyal
Pinks
Rue
Pineapple sage
Fragrant thymes
Winter green
Woodruff

Planting and growing herbs

Plant a herb garden within view of the kitchen window to give the cook inspiration.

A clay soil, light in texture and well managed is perfectly suited to the cultivation of herbs.

Make the sunniest and most sheltered part of the garden into the herb plot as winds dry the herbs and take away some of their scent and flavour.

Put the herbs that grow tallest at the back of the plot where they will not interfere with the growth of the lower ones.

Fennel must be put at the back
Above the lower plants it towers,
The fennel with its yellow flowers.

Also said of fennel
Sow fennel, sow sorrow.

Cats will leave catmint alone if it is grown from seed:
If you set it, cats will eat it;
If you sow it, cats don't know it.

Alecost won't flower if it is grown in the shade.

Basill is sowen in gardens in earthen pots.

Keep basil and rue apart as each retards the other's growth.

Basil needs hot sun in order to thrive.

Only sow a few seeds of chervil at a time throughout the summer as it flowers and bolts quickly.

Chives will grow in any garden.

Plant garlic bulbs in a sunny spot.

Where the sage tree thrives and grows,
The master's not master, and that he knows.

Sage, rosemary and lavender are all feminine plants that are said to flourish 'wher the missus is master'.

Add soot to the soil when you grow parsley.

Sow parsley in April, July and February for a year round crop.

Renew parsley beds every two years.

Curled parsley is more susceptible to the cold and damp, so grow it in a protecting frame.

Parsley is one of the most difficult of herbs to grow. It was thought that it was best sown with curses on Good Friday when you came home from church. You would be sure it came up then but even so it went nine times to the Devil and back again first.

The marigold is said to bloom on the calends of every month.

If mint plants get 'mint disease' dig them up and don't use the ground for mint again for several years.

Rosemary grows smaller on chalk soil, but is more fragrant.

Winter savory is woodier and bushier than the summer variety.

Tarragon is best raised by division of the roots.

The perfume of lemon thyme is sweeter if it is raised from cuttings.

Thyme is a faithful companion of the lavender. It lives with it in perfect sympathy and partakes alike of its good and bad fortune.

Thyme quickly uses up the goodness in the soil, so manure well if you dig it up and wish to replace it with something else.

Balm grows well in any soil.

A camomile bed,
The more it is trodden,
The more it will spread.

Grow camomile all round the garden to give health to other plants.

Wormwood likes the shade.

Southernwood rarely flowers in England.

Grow hyssop with catmint in a border.

Pennyroyal grows best in damp places and near water.

Grow woodruff under fruit trees.

Harvesting and drying herbs

Gather herbs when the sap is full in the top of them. Such herbs as you intend to gather for drying, to keep them for use all the winter, do it about Lammastide (1 August); dry them in the shade that the sun draw not out their virtue, but in a clear air and breezy wind, that no mustiness may taint them.

Herbs for drying must be gathered at full moon.

Lift roots in the autumn when the leaves begin to die back.

Make sure leaves are insect and disease free.

Don't pick leaves with a heavy dew or rain on them.

When collecting the seeds allow them to ripen as much as possible. Break off the stems and hang them upside down with a paper bag over the flowerhead.

Dry leaves and flowers in a dry, warm, airy spot.

Bunches should only be made up of a few sprigs.

Herbs put in warm, direct sunlight to dry will be bleached and their flavour will diminish.

Store dried herbs in light and airtight jars.

Soft fruits

The soft fruit season is only a very short one but it is well worth caring all year for plants that are going to provide you with the treats of summer.

Virgin land is always the best for strawberries.

In September
Wife, into thy garden, and set me a plot,
With strawberry rootes, of the best to be got:
Such growing abroade, among thornes in the wood,
Wel chosen and picked prove excellent good.

The Barbery, Respis and Gooseberry too,
Looke now to be planted as other things doo:
The Gooseberry, Respis, and Roses, all three,
With Strawberries under them trimly agree.

In December
If frost doe continue, take this for a lawe,
The strawberries looke to be covered with straw.
Laid overly trim upon crotchis and bows,
And after uncovered, as weather allows.

Strawberry plants set in July are ready for picking the following summer. If you set them in September, pinch out the flowers the first summer and wait another year.

The first yield of a strawberry plant is always the best.

The most popular varieties of strawberries now are Red Gauntlet and Cambridge Favourite.

For soft fruits you need rain in useful quantities delivered over short periods.

Blackcurrants crop on new wood, redcurrants on old.

Pick blackcurrants on a hot summer's day when the air is full of their scent.

Garden pests

Destroying pests with chemicals upsets the balance of nature and harms the soil. There are far better ways of controlling them naturally.

Moles
Put holly, gorse or broken glass down their holes.
Grow caper spurge in the garden.
Find the largest mole hill, dig down until you can see the tunnel running in both directions and put in a cut bulb of garlic or strong onion.
(It is said that if there are numerous mole hills in the garden the owner owes money!)

Rats
They dislike catmint so grow it round the plants they attack.

Slugs
Boil artemisia and rue, strain off the water and spray your plants with it.
Strip the leaves from Brussels sprouts and lay them on the ground to draw the slugs away from the leaves on the plant.
Lay prickly thistles or bracken between the plants.
Sink a bowl of beer in the ground. The slugs will be attracted by it and fall in and drown. Replace the beer once a week.

Greenfly
Spray plants with liquid seaweed.
Grow chives or parsley amongst plants that are likely to be affected.
Make an effective spray by soaking nettles in rainwater for three weeks.

Whitefly
Keep it away both in and out of the greenhouse by growing marigolds and nasturtiums amongst plants likely to be affected.

Blackfly
A spray can be made by making a decoction of artemisia, tomato leaves and nettles. Dilute it and add liquid seaweed.
Deter blackfly from eating the sap of spring-sown broad beans by spraying with liquid seaweed; keep it away from autumn sown beans by pinching them out.

Cabbage root fly
If there is enough humus in the soil the cabbage roots should be so large that he can eat his fill without doing any damage to the plant.

Carrot fly
After hoeing, sprinkle the ground with dried wormwood, hyssop, mugwort or southernwood. The fly will be attracted to these instead of the carrots.
Sow parsley or any member of the onion family amongst the carrots to disguise the smell.

Onion fly
Sow the onions from sets instead of seed.
If you do use seed, plant parsley nearby.

White butterfly
Grow fragrant herbs near the cabbages such as: hyssop, sage, thyme, mint, artemisias, rosemary.

Caterpillar
Compost grown plants can withstand caterpillar damage with no lasting effect. Spray cabbages (but not cauliflower or broccoli) with sea-water.

Moths
Grow southernwood near all plants likely to be attacked.

Ants
Repel them by growing tansy or pennyroyal.

Flea beetle
(attacks cucumber, radish, marrow and cabbage):
Mulch the plants with elderberry leaves and flowers or grow strong, aromatic plants nearby such as mint.

Millipedes:
(attacks bean and pea seeds):
Scatter dried and powdered aromatic plants in the bed with the seeds.
Better still, raise the plants indoors and set them out.

Wire worms
Make a trap by getting an old can, punching it full of holes and filling it with potato peelings. Empty it every few weeks.

Mildew
Scatter dried marestail on the ground round plants likely to be affected.
Spray the plants with liquid seaweed.

Fungus on potatoes and tomatoes
Spray them with a decoction of marestail.

Wood pigeons
Hang up red flags or sacks.

All birds
Prevent your plants from being eaten, by scattering dried, powdered garlic round them.

Do not destroy
bats – they eat the insects that eat your plants.
bees – they pollinate your plants and provide you with honey.
the Devils Coach Horse and Tiger beetles – they eat destroying insects.
the Violet Ground beetle – he eats slugs and caterpillars
centipedes – they eat grubs, slugs and insects.
the earthworm – he is man's most valuable garden helper as he turns the soil for you.

If there were more gowks (cuckoos) there would be better crops in the fields and more fruit in the gardens, because the cuckoo is as fond of hairyworms and caterpillars as the blackbird is of gooseberries.

Trees

Even though we have plastics and other modern materials, wood is still one of the most durable and is certainly the most attractive. Every tree has its use, be it the great oak or the tiny wayfaring tree. Trees grace the countryside and eventually our homes and are put to work in all manner of ways.

Save elm, ash and crabtree, for cart and for plough,
Save step for a stile, of the crotch of a bough,

Save hazel for forks, save sallow for rake,
Save hulver and thorne, thereof flail for to make.

Of all the trees that grow so fair,
Old England to adorn,
Greater are none beneath the sun,
Than oak and ash and thorn.

Oak

Oak of the clay lived many a day
Or ever Aeneas began.

The oak is the first tree in the forest.

The flower is known as the tail and the oak-apple as the sheets-axe.

Fell an oak tree in winter to get the best grain.

Oak makes the best gates: they will last for over a century if fastened with wooden pegs instead of iron.

Oak is impervious to alcohol so it is used for beer barrels and wine casks.

Oak sawdust gives the best flavour to smoked hams and kippers.
Tannin extracted from the bark is used for tanning hides.

Other uses
weatherboarding on the outside of buildings
timbers inside buildings (they must be pegged together as they are difficult to nail)
the keel, frame and ribs of sailing ships
coracle ribs
church pews and pulpits
staircases
panelling
ladder rungs
cartwheel spokes, and the framework of carts
bar or rail fencing
windmill wheels

the water wheel of a watermill
slats of garden trugs.

The root stump can be used as an anvil base.

Ash
Ash of the loam was a lady at home,
When Brut was an outlaw man.

Ash timber is white with a pale brown heart.

Ash wood is tough and supple and doesn't splinter.

An ash joist will bear more before it breaks than any other tree.

Ash makes elegant furniture as it bends easily after steaming and takes a high polish.

Uses
frames, shafts and wooden wheel-rims of carts
handles of picks, axes, hammers and garden tools
hurdles
poles, stakes and hop-poles
bean rods and pea sticks
slats of garden trugs
oars
tennis racquets and skis
arrow shafts
walking sticks
Welsh shepherd's crooks, using the root for the curve
crates
some types of clogs worn in the North
ash bark has been used for tanning nets.

Hawthorn
Thorn of the Down saw New Troy Town
(From which was London born.)

Where the soil is rich enough and deep enough to support it, the main use of the hawthorn is for hedging.

Young trees are planted 22·5 cm (9 in) apart to make a hedge. Hawthorn timber is used for hedge stakes and to make the wooden cudgels for driving them in.

The hawthorn is the mother of the oak and the ash. (The hedge gives shelter to the growing seedlings.)

Hawthorn provides food and shelter for the birds.

Young hawthorn leaves in April make a tasty addition to suet puddings.

Witness hearby the ancientry
Of Oak and Ash and Thorn.

In times of storm
Beware of an oak,
It courts the stroke.
Avoid an ash,
It courts the flash,
Creep under a thorn,
It will save you from harm.

Yew

Yew that is old in churchyard mould, He breedeth a mighty bow.

Yew timber is slower growing than oak and is as hard.

Yew wood resists the action of water.

Yew has a fine-looking grain.

The seeds of the berries are poisonous but not the flesh.

The cut, withered leaves are poisonous to animals.

Uses
bows
barrel hoops
the bows, backs and arms of cottage furniture, particularly Windsor chairs

Alder
Alder for shoes do some men choose.

Alder is a yellow wood, hard and easily carved.

Alder stands up well to water.

Uses
clogs and shoes
pumps, troughs and sluices
broom and tool handles
bowls and spoons
herring barrel staves

The roots and knots are used for cabinet-making.

Charcoal from the twigs makes excellent gunpowder.

Beech
And beech for cups also.

Beech wood is iron-hard when seasoned but not durable outside.

Beech roots allow a good circulation of air through the soil and any other trees planted near will benefit.

When green, beech is easily turned and it is made into legs and spars for Windsor-type chairs.

Uses
cogs on mill-wheels
clogs for wearing in wet places such as tanneries and laundries
saddle-trees
boot lasts
woodworking planes and tools
wooden bowls
granary shovels

Elm

Ellum she hates mankind, and waits
  Till every gust be laid
To drop a limb on the head of him
  That anyway trusts her shade.
(The elm has a reputation for suddenly dropping a branch for no apparent reason.)

If rooks destroy their nest in an elm tree, the branch on which it rested will soon fall.

If rooks desert an elm, the tree will soon fall.

Elm wood is strong and tough but only if it is kept wet.

If you saw it right, elm wood looks dappled like the breast of a partridge.

Elm wood has a twisting grain and won't splinter.

Elm wood must be seasoned for one year for every inch of its thickness.

Elm wood is good for carving.

Uses
ships' timber
wheel hubs
undercarriages of carts
the inside of carts and wheelbarrows
sides of barns
bakers' dough troughs
outdoor furniture
chair seats and table tops for cottage furniture
lock gates
water pumps and pipes
coffins

The elm tod (the knotty growth that sometimes forms on the trunk) is studded with nails and used to make a heavy, wooden mallet called a 'beetle'.

Willow

Known also as withy, sallow, sollar or sally.

The willow could buy a horse
Before the oak could pay for his saddle.

Be the oak ne'er so stout,
The sollar red will wear it out.

In lopping old Iocham, for fear of mishap,
One bough stay unlopped, to cherish the sap.
The second year after then boldly ye may.
For dipping his fellows, that bough cut away.

Uses

boat paddles and propellers
cricket bats
cradles and cribs
artificial limbs
yokes for carrying milk pails and baskets (as it is strong and light)
slats of garden trugs
gate hurdles

Willow wands are woven to make baskets and hampers, lobster and crab pots, eel-hives, bird cages and pet baskets.

Birch

The birch is called the Lady of the Woods.

After rain, birch trees smell sweet.

Birch wood is hard, but not durable outside.

Uses

cotton reels and bobbins
tool and broom handles
spoons
frames of garden trugs
cottage furniture

The twigs are bound into besom heads and have been used in thatching.

Walnut

A woman, a spaniel and a walnut tree,
The more you beat 'em the better they be.

If a tree doesn't bear nuts, beat it in March when the sap is rising.

'... leaves spread themselves far abroad ... the catkins or aglets come forth before the nuts: these Nuts doe grow hard to the stalke of the leaves, by couples or by three and three ... the inner pulpe whereof is white, sweet and pleasant to the taste.'

One walnut tree can yield 68 kg (150 lb) of nuts a year.

Walnut trees can take a hundred years to reach maturity. Walnut wood is attractively grained, hard, shock absorbent and valuable. It is even-textured and does not warp or shrink.

Burr walnut is made from the growth of incipient twigs on the trunk.

Uses
cabinet-making and fine furniture
aeroplane propellers
stocks of sporting guns
turned egg-cups, cruets and peppermills.

Hazel

Left to their own devices hazel trees produce small round nuts that can be picked from late August.

If hazel trees are cut back every seven years they send up a mass of slender, straight shoots. These are used more than the wood from the trunk.

Uses
spars, runners and pegs for thatching
pea sticks and bean rods
cask hoops
crates for pottery
woven sheep hurdles
walking sticks

The wood is used for small stakes and clothes props.

Hazel wood makes good charcoal.

Hazel coppices provide excellent cover for game birds.

To find water with a hazel rod
Find a forked hazel twig and hold the thin arms with your fingers and thumbs. Walk slowly over a suspected water source and if water is below the twig should jerk upwards. If you are a born diviner the rod becomes vibrant and often goes round in a circle, breaking off at the short points. The twig will lie motionless if you are an unsympathetic person whether water is there or not.

Sweet chestnut
The fruite is enclosed in a rough and prickly huske like to an hedgehog or urchin.

Mature chestnut timber is the colour of oak, but it is hard to saw and has the 'shakes' (natural cracks) so it is rarely used for large planks.

Chestnuts are usually coppiced and cut every twelve years for one hundred years.

Uses
cleft-pale fencing
hop poles
gate hurdles
gate posts
pit props
wine barrels

The leaves and shoots of chestnut are good fodder for goats and sheep and the dried leaves make excellent litter for stabling.

Dried chestnut leaves are a good addition to the compost heap.

Sycamore

Sycamore wood is strong, but not durable outside.
It is pale cream and stainproof.

Uses

white kitchenware such as bread and cheese boards, rolling pins and platters

carved woodware
table tops
draining boards
rollers of old-fashioned mangles
textile rollers
the back, sides and stock of violins

Spindle tree

Before the spinning wheel came into use, the thin stems of the spindle tree were used to make spindles for spinning wool. Gypsies call it skewer-wood as from it they make skewers, knitting needles and clothes pegs.

Lime

Lime wood is firm, white, close-grained and smooth.

It is the best wood for intricate carving.

Uses

hat blocks
shoe trees
piano keys

The outer bark comes off in fibres which can be used by gardeners for tying bundles and plants.

The fibres can be made into a coarse matting.

A fragrant tea can be made from the flowers.

Hornbeam
The hornbeam is the hardest of hardwood trees.

Hornbeam wood is too hard for the craftsman.

Uses
cogs in water and windmill machinery
mallets
carpenters' plane blocks
large wooden screws
ox yokes
the moving parts of pianos
butchers' chopping blocks
bowls
planks of threshing floors

Rowan (Mountain ash)
Rowan wood is a dark red-brown and is as tough as its berries are bitter.

It is used for tool handles and small turned or carved objects.

Elder (Pipe tree, Bour tree, Ellan)
Bour tree, bour tree: crooked rong,
Never straight and never strong;
Ever bush and never tree
Since Our Lord was nailed on thee.

Elder is the Tree of Disgrace.

It was once thought to be the home of the elder witch who should be treated with respect:
When felling an elder, say:
Owd girl, give me of thy wood,

An' I will give thee some of mine
When I grow into a tree.

As one elder dies, another grows up.

An elder stake lasts longer in the ground than an iron bar.

An elder stake and a blackthorn ether
Will make a hedge last forever.
(An ether is a flexible piece of wood wound between the main stakes when laying a hedge.)

Elder wood is white and hard and polishes well.

Uses
fine picks for cleaning the insides of watches
skewers
carved combs
needles for weaving fishing nets
tops of fishing rods
chessmen

The twigs can be hollowed out and made into pea-shooters and whistles (hence, Pipe tree).

Small toys can be carved from the pith.

Blackthorn
Blackthorn stems, trimmed and polished so they are black and shiny, make walking sticks.
The cudgel known as a shillalagh is made from the stout, rough stems. A leather strap is fixed to it so it can hang from the wrist.

Wayfaring tree (Hoarwithy)
The twigs are supple and easily twisted and can be used for tying bundles.

Dogwood
When dogwood is cut back it sends out many coppice shoots.

Uses
spokes
bobbins
toothpicks
skewers
mill clogs

Box
Box wood is orange-brown, hard and even-grained.

Uses
fine carving and engraving
chessmen and other small, decorative objects
mathematical instruments such as scales and rulers

The root is likewise yellow and harder than the timber, but of greater beauty.

Cropping trees
Cut trees in the waxing of the moon and the poles (new branche will grow out straighter.

Felling trees
Other terms for felling: falling; throwing.

Trees are best felled at the waning of the moon and when the wind is in the north.

Timber should be felled on the bating of the moon, because the sap is then down, and the wood will be more durable.

If you fell trees to sell to the carpenter, don't do it at full moon or the wood will be soft and tender, subject also to worms and putrefaction, and that quickly, by reason of excessive moisture.

Method of felling
Laying in. The buttresses or swellings leading to the roots are felled with an axe.

A tapering gap is cut in the 'face' of the trunk, i.e. the side of the tree facing the direction in which you want it to fall. The 'back' of the tree (the opposite side) is sawn through. Where sawing is done by hand with a two-man saw, each man alternately pulls and releases and all the work is done on the pull-stroke.

If a tree is wrongly felled it can split from top to bottom with a loud crack as it falls, because the tension at the base has been wrongly released.

4 The weather

Weather lore

The daily life of the countryman has always been affected by the weather. It governs the outside jobs he can accomplish, the sowing, growing and harvesting of his crops and the health and welfare of himself, his family and his animals.

Weather calendar

If you look at the first twelve days of January and make them represent the successive months you will be able to predict the weather for the coming year.

If January calends be summerly gay,
'Twill be wintry weather till the calends of May.

If on the 12 January the sun shine,
It foreshadows much wind.

If Candlemas Day be bright and clear,
There'll be two winters in one year;
But if Candlemas Day be thick with rain,
Winter is gone and won't come again.

If the birds sing at Candlemas, they will cry before May.

Where the wind blows on Candlemas Eve,
There it will stay until May Eve.

There is always one fine week in February.

Where the wind is on 21 March (the vernal equinox) there it will stay until 21 June (the summer solstice).

As many mists in March you see,
So many frosts in May will be.

If March comes in like a lion, it goes out like a lamb.
If it comes in like a lamb it goes out like a lion.

If the first three days of April be foggy,
Rain in June will make the lanes boggy.

Who doffs his coat on a Winter's day,
Will gladly put it on in May.

In the middle of May comes the tail of winter.

No wind is colder than a May wind.

A wet June makes a dry September.

If the first of July be rainy weather,
It will rain, more or less, for four weeks together.

St Swithin's Day if thou be fair
For forty days 'twill rain no more.
St Swithin's Day if thou bring rain
For forty days it will remain.
(St Swithin's Day is 15 July)

All the tears St Swithin can cry,
St Bartlemy's mantle wipes 'em dry.
(24 August is St Bartholomew's Day)

Fair weather on St Giles Day, fair for the rest of the month.
(St Giles Day is 1 September)

Whatever the weather on 8 September, it will last for the next four weeks.

So many days old the moon is on Michaelmas Day (29 September), so many floods after.

28 October is always rainy.

For every fog in October, a snow in the winter, heavy or light according as the fog is heavy or light.

If ducks do swim at Hallontide,
At Christmas they will slide.
(Hallontide is 11 November)

Ice in November enough to bear a duck,
Nought else all year excepting slush and muck.

If the ice will bear a man before Christmas,
It won't bear a goose after.

On 21 December (St Thomas's Day and the winter solstice) whatever direction the wind blows at noon it will stay for the next lunar quarter.

Predicting by the time of day

If it rains before seven,
It will be dry before eleven.

If the sun rises early in the morning and quickly goes to bed again, the rest of the day will be dull.

Between the hours of twelve and two
You'll see what the day will do.

Predicting by the sky

A wary eye cast up at the sky can often help you to decide whether or not to take a raincoat out with you.

Evening red and morning grey,
Sends the traveller on his way.
Evening grey and morning red,
Sends the traveller wet to bed.
The 'red sky' rhymes have always told us the same, but a red sky at any time will tell you bad weather is to follow, not immediately, but within the next twenty-four hours.

If the grey 'shepherd's flocks' (puffy grey clouds) appear first thing in the morning, there will be rain before nightfall.

Small clouds scudding in front of large ones are called water carts and when they appear, rain is to come.

Puffy white cotton-wool clouds (fair weather cumulus) occurring later in the morning show that the weather will be fine with a light breeze.

Cirrus clouds (small whispy ones) are a sign of stormy weather to come.

Low stratus clouds are thick and grey. Rain is either here or on the way and may last for several days.

Long banks of stratus clouds over sea cliffs will produce hill fog and eventually rain.

When stratus clouds begin to break up they become strato-cumulus, and the weather should get finer and slightly warmer.

The white anvil (cumulo-nimbus) brings downpours and storms.

The mackerel or cruddly sky (cirro-cumulus) marks the end of unsettled weather.

Mackerel sky,
Twelve hours dry.

although also you find
If there be a cruddly sky,
It's neither long for wet nor dry.

Mackerel skies and colt's tails*
Make big ships carry little sails.

When aeroplane trails won't go away it will be cloudy and humid, and there may be fog.

Rainbow in th'marnin'
Gies the shepherd warnin'
To car' his girt coat on his back.
Rainbow at night be shepherd's delight,
For then no girt coat will be lack.

Broken parts of a rainbow are called weather-dogs, wind-hogs or weather-galls and denote blustery weather.

The wind

Every wind has its weather.

* cirrus

The weather's always ill
When the wind's not still.

A north wind is a broom for the channel.

A northern air brings fair weather.

When the wind's in the East,
It's neither fit for man nor beast.

or
It rains for twenty-four hours at least.

When the wind's in the South
It is in the rain's mouth.

A western wind carries water in its hand.

A west wind north about,
Never long holds out.

North wind brings hail,
South wind brings rain,
East winds we bewail,
West winds blow amain,
North-east wind is too cold,
South-east wind, not too warm,
North-west wind is far too bold,
South-west wind doth no harm.

The moon and stars and the weather
If the moon on Saturday be new or full,
There always was rain and there always will.

The new moon always brings a change in the weather.

An underground moon brings bad weather. (A moon that changes between midnight and 1 a.m.)

Sharp horns mean windy weather.

The moon on its back
Holds rain in its lap.

There will be wild weather if there is a bright star dogging the moon.

If there are mists in the new moon there will be rain in the old,
If there are mists in the old moon there will be rain in the new.

If the moon shows like a silver shield,
You needn't be afraid to reap your field;
But if she rises haloed round,
Soon we'll tread on deluged ground.

The full moons clears the sky.

Weather signs from birds and animals

It is possible that birds and animals are sensitive to atmospheric pressure that we cannot feel, and so their behaviour can tell us something of the approaching weather.

There will be rain if
blackbirds cry unusually shrilly;
a robin sings in the morning or sings in the bottom of a bush;
swallows and martins fly low;
jackdaws flutter and caw round the church steeple or if they are late coming home to roost;
rooks fly low, stay near their rookeries or never leave their nests;
magpies nests are built high;
a woodpecker cries loudly.

It will be fine if
swallows and martins fly high;
rooks go foraging far afield and fly high;
skylarks fly high (the higher they go the better the weather).

Seagull, seagull, get on the sand,
It's never fine weather when you're on the land.

It will be stormy if partridges rise and fall in coveys and eventually congregate; and if pheasants make for cover and stay perched on low branches of hedges and trees.

There will be rain if hens huddle together forlornly or if the cockerel oversleeps; and if geese congregate together and honk.

Pigs can see the wind and become restless before high winds and storms.

Horses get restless and shake their heads just before rain.

Sheep will lie down peacefully and quietly if the weather is going to be fine and will often lie still until well into the mornin When they get up and graze early or huddle together by bushes and trees, then expect rain.
Rain on the way makes sheep bleat for no apparent reason. If they do this in a long, dry spell the weather will soon break.

When all the cattle lie down together in low pastures and face the wind, then it will be wet.
When they move to higher ground and stand at rest it will be fine.
Cattle can sense thunderstorms brewing and become restless and uneasy and run round the pasture.

If the cat turns her back to the fire there will be a frost. If she suddenly decides to run about, play like a kitten and scratch at the furniture the weather will be rough and stormy.

Black beetles are a sign of rain and to kill them brings a downpour.

If spiders' webs are short and broken, or there are a few of them rain is coming.

Bees like fine weather and fly far afield collecting pollen. If they stay close to their hives, expect rain.

Telling the weather by flowers, plants and trees
The scarlet pimpernel is the 'poor man's weather glass' – it opens its tiny flowers before a fine spell and closes them before rain.

There will be rain if
clover stands upright;

convolvulous flowers close;
the flower of the cinquefoil opens.

Onions skin very thin,
Mild winter coming in;
Onions skin thick and tough,
Coming winter will be rough.

15 November
If on the trees the leaves still hold,
The coming winter will be cold.

The oak and the ash tell of the coming summer:
If the oak before the ash,
There will only be a splash;

If the ash before the oak,
Then we're sure to get a soak.

Many haws,
Many sloes,
Many cold toes.

Many holly berries, cold winter.

However much we try to predict the weather, it always seems to trick us in the end. Perhaps the only sound weather sayings are:
Fools are weatherwise.

Those that are weatherwise
Are rarely otherwise.

Let no such vulgar tables debase thy mind,
Nor Paul nor Swithin rule the clouds and wind.

Well, Duncomb, what will be the weather?
Sir, it looks cloudy altogether.
And coming 'cross our Houghton Green
I stopp'd and talked with old Franke Beane.
While we stood there, sir, old Jon Swain
Went by and said he know'd 'twould rain.
The next that came was Master Hunt,
And he declar'd he knew it won't.

And then I met with Farmer Blow,
He told me plainly he di'nt know:
So, sir, when doctors disagree
Who's to decide it, you or me?

5 Country fare

Baking bread

Without bread all is misery.

Bread is the pledge of peace and happiness in the labourer's dwelling.

What a pleasure it is to make bread: to watch the yeast start to work, to knead it into the flour with an easy rhythm, to set the dough to rise and to come back to it an hour later to find it has doubled in size as if by magic. Then to shape and to prove it, and bake it until it is golden and crusty on the outside and soft and crumbly in the middle. How satisfying it all is and, when the loaves are standing to cool on their racks, 'what can be pleasanter to behold?'

How wasteful and indeed how shameful, for a labourer's wife to go to the baker's shop; and how negligent, how criminally careless of the welfare of his family, must the labourer be, who permits so scandalous a use of the proceeds of his labour.

A servant that cannot make bread is not entitled to the same wages as one who can.

Enjoy making bread – the more you worry about it, the less success you are likely to have.

Bad feelings make bad bread.

Ingredients for bread
good wholemeal flour
a little salt
the whey left over from making butter or cheese (or plain water)
the yeast left over from brewing

What I would recommend to gentlemen with considerable families, or to farmers, is a mill.
(The mill recommended by Cobbett was a horse-mill. Now you can buy electric ones.)

The finest flour is by no means the most wholesome.

Dried yeast is better than stale 'fresh' yeast.

Yeast is living, so treat it kindly. (Don't scald it.)

Test the temperature of the liquid with your little finger – it is less hard-worked than the rest.

A teaspoon of Ascension Day rain added to the dough makes it light.

Adding too much water to the dough was called 'putting the miller's eye out'.

Knead the bread with a constant and easy rhythm.

The dough must be well worked. The fists must go heartily into it. It must be rolled over and pressed out, folded up and pressed out again, until it be completely mixed, and formed into a stiff and tough dough.

If the bread turned out small and hard it was sometimes called 'slut-farthings' or 'lazy-backs' as it was thought it hadn't been kneaded properly.

A cross-cut on top of the dough will help it rise. (Traditionally it kept out the power of witches and devils who would prevent the bread from rising.)

Dough will not rise on a thundery day.

Dough rises best at full moon.

Bread shapes
cottage – divide the dough into one-third and two-thirds and make two fairly flat rounds. Put the smaller on top of the larger and make a hole down through the two.
round or cob – form the dough into a fairly high round so it won't spread out flat as it cooks.

scone – usually made with soda bread. It is formed like a round loaf, with a cross on the top.
bakestone – make a round loaf and turn it over once during cooking after it has started to rise.
tin – punch the dough down into a bread tin.
square tin – use a bread tin with a flat lid.
round tin – usually only available from bakers. It is baked in a closed round tin.
bloomer – long, fairly thick loaf, made by forming the dough into a high long-shape (although not as long as a French loaf) and scoring the top with diagonal cuts.
Sally Lunn or teabread – use a 12 cm (5 in) diameter round cake tin to each 225 g (½ lb) flour.
pot loaf – bake it in a thick stone jar.
flower pot – bake it in a flower pot.
plait – make three sausage-shapes, join them at one end, plait them twice and join them at the other end.

Bread baked without tins in a brick oven tastes better, as pieces of charcoal stick to the sides.

To give bread baked in a modern oven a 'brick' flavour, bake the loaves in flower pots. Season the pots first by greasing them well with lard and baking them at a high temperature. Do this several times and after this never wash them.

A cross was often cut in the top of the bread, again to keep out witches. If this were not done the bread would be 'sad' (not risen) or 'ropy' (uneatable), or burnt.

To guard against ropiness hang a piece of ropy bread on the bacon rack on Good Friday and leave it there for a year.

Unrisen bread is also said to have 'gone dumpy'.

Oven temperature
Women who understand the matter, know when the heat is right the moment they put their faces within a yard of the oven mouth.

Putting the loaves in the oven is called 'setting in'. It should be done calmly and quickly and everything else should be disregarded until it is finished.

Only one person should put the bread in the oven – if two do it, they will quarrel.

During baking, do not look at the bread in order to see how it is going on.

Bread must not be cut with a knife while the next batch is in the oven, although it may be broken.

Don't overcook or undercook
Much dowbake I praise not, much crust is as ill.

If the bread is still singing when you put your ear to it, it isn't yet done.

Take the bread from the oven quickly, one loaf at a time.

Take the bread from the tins as soon as possible.

New bread is a waste, but mouldy is worse:
What Dog getteth that way, that looseth thy purse.

Don't waste bread
You will be hungry if you throw bread on the fire.

Stand back and be pleased with your new batch of bread
Here is cut and come again. Here is bread always for the table. Bread to carry afield; always a hunch of bread to put into the hand of a hungry child.

Cider

And every man drink up his cup,
Here's health to the old apple tree.

Cider was made more on farms in apple-growing counties than in the home. When wages were often paid in kind, it was an economical drink for the farmer to give to his workers as it allowed him to keep all his barley for sending to market. Some farms had their own cider press, but very often there was one shared between a whole district that was trundled round from farm to farm from late autumn to Christmas.

Making cider is a much simpler process than brewing beer or country wine. All you need are apples, something to pulp and press them with and a wooden barrel.

To make rough cider
Pulp the apples.
Press out the juice.
Put the juice into wooden barrels and leave them to stand in the orchard for six months.

When to press
Traditionally, cider-making began on All Saints' Day (1 November). Apple-pressing now begins in September and most of the work is done between then and Christmas. Pressing carries on until March if there are still enough apples.

On 19, 20 and 21 May there are often frosts that destroy the next crop of cider apples. These are said to occur because a Devon brewer called Franklin sold his soul to the Devil for frost on those three days to destroy the apples so people would buy his beer. Another story is that all the brewers of North Devon promised the Devil they would adulterate their beer in exchange for frosts on those days.

Cider apples
Cider apples are not fit for eating, with the exception of an old Devon variety known as 'stire-apple'.

Names of cider apples
Kentish Pippins, Herefordshire Styne, Warrenden (or Quarenden), Rusticoats, Cowley Crabs, White Swan, Culverings, French Longtails, Redstreak, Rubystreak, Longstreak-Redstreak.

Nowadays, most cider is made from the rejects from pack houses, not the bad ones but the small or misshapen apples.

The best apples for cider today are Bramleys or a mixture of Bramleys and Laxtons.

Cider apples should be given time to weather and mature. Whe they are used they should be turning yellow and beginning to wrinkle.

Pressing the apples
Don't let metal touch the fruit.

In a large press the pulp is put between layers of hessian and wickerwork mats. On a smaller scale, you can use an old-fashioned mangle.

In the barrel
Put the juice directly into wooden barrels.

A good cider should rely solely on the apples from which it is made – you should not have to add anything. (Although all kinds of 'improvers' by way of blood, milk or cream, a resin-soaked rag, or even a dead sheep are said to have been used.)

Never add water to the apple juice, but if you wash the pulp through with fresh water you will have a light drink suitable fo children and excellent for cooking.

No sugar should be added to rough cider. Its sweetness was once determined by the type of apple used, and its strength wa that which a good fermentation of the natural apple juice woul yield.

Sweet cider was once made by adding a piece of burning brimstone to the cask as the apple juice fermented, but this isn't to be recommended as you can taste the sulphuric acid.

Never filter cider, just leave the cask undisturbed so the golden liquid can be naturally cleared by the frosts.

Hold your ear to the cider cask and you can hear the cider singing gently to itself.

An English drink

There is no waste when you make cider – you take windfall apples, press them to make the best drink of all and then the cake left over is fed to bullocks or pigs. It is one of our English traditional drinks. Why, then, do we pay as much duty as there is on French wines? (Kentish cider-maker)

Vintage cider

Vintage cider is made with sugar and is left to mature far longer than rough cider.

Drinking the cider

Rough cider in the West Country was drunk from a cider jug, which was larger than 6 dl (1 pint). The drinkers' jugs were replenished from one holding 9 litres (2 gallons).

Local name for cider in Somerset: Tanglefoot, because of what it does to you on the way home.

Round the rick, and round the rick,
There I met my Uncle Dick.
I cut off his head and drank his blood,
And left his body Standing.
What was he?
A bottle of cider.

Beer on cider makes a bad rider,
Cider on beer makes good cheer.

Then fill up the jug, boys, and let it go round,
Of drinks not the equal in England is found.
So pass round the jug, boys, and pull at it free,
There's nothing like cider, rough cider, for me.

Brewing beer

Ale or beer

Generous wine is for the Court,
The Citie calls for Beere!
But Ale! Bonny Ale! Like a Lord of the Soyle!
In the Countrey shall domineere!

When hops were first introduced into Britain around 1520, the traditional drink in country and town was ale, which was brewe with malt and yeast only, and flavoured with herbs. Hops were rejected by many people at first and their use was even banned by Henry VIII who loved spiced ale. Gradually, it became evident that they were the best ingredient for both flavouring and preserving malt liquor and they were universally accepted. In many country households, however, wild herbs were easier come by than hops and so ale was still brewed for a time.

Eventually, brewing with hops became the norm and the two words, ale and beer, became interchangeable.

Oh, Good Ale, thou art my darling;
Thou art my joy both night and morning.

Stay, traveller, come in here,
Here's bread and cheese and good old beer.

Home brewing

Where brewing is needful, be brewer thyselfe.

At one time to have a house and not to brew was a rare thing indeed.

The twice-yearly brewing was once as common in every household as the weekly baking, and these days, with the price of beer going up every year, more and more people are taking to brewing their own.

In buying thy drink, by the firkin or pot,
The score doth arise, the hogge profiteth not.

The beer should always suit the occasion and so two, or perhaps more types of varying strengths were made at each brewing. There was a very weak one for the children, and the next, only a little stronger, was the 'small beer' for the harvest workers. Theirs was thirsty work and they needed a quantity of liquid without being fuddled with alcohol.

When a man is mowing, reaping, or is at any other hard work, 1 litre (1 quart), or 1.5 litres (3 pints) of really good ale a day is by no means too much.

The strongest beer was made for special occasions, the most important being Christmas. This was usually made in October with the new malt from the summer's barley.

The other brewing was usually in March, April or May. Summer was thought to be a bad time for brewing as hot, thundery weather makes beer flat and vinegary.

When elder is white, brew and bake a peck.
When elder is black, brew and bake a sack.

Both beer and ale are apt to be foul, disturbed and flat in the bean season.

Bow-wow, dandy-fly
Brew no beer in July.

Basic ingredients of beer
1 bushel malt
450 g (1 lb) hops
6 dl (1 pint) yeast
good water

One bushel, well brewed, out lasteth some twaine.

Malt

. . . to make thine own mault, it shall profit thee much.

If your brewing be considerable in amount, grind your own malt.

Malt is made by steeping barley grains in water so they begin to germinate, and then heating them so the process stops and they dry. The longer they are heated, the darker the malt and, consequently, the beer.

Mault being well dried the longer will last.

Unmalted barley produces strength but the beer is flat.

Barley is heavier than malt.

To discover what proportion of your barley is unmalted, put a handful into cold water. The grains that sink are no good.

Hops

The manifold vertues of Hops do manifestly argue the wholesomeness of beers above ale; for the hops rather make it a physical drinke and keepe the body in good health, than an ordinary drinke for quenching the thirst.

The hop for his profit, I thus do exalt
It strengtheneth drink and it favoureth malt:
And being well brewed long kept it will last,
And drawing abide if ye draw not too fast.

Hops preserve beer and give it a pleasant bitter flavour.

Hops should be bright and have no leaves or bits of branches amongst them.

They should not be brown but a fresh green. They should have a clammy feel when rubbed between the fingers, and a pleasant smell.

Hops retain their preserving qualities for a considerable time, but their flavour begins to go at a year old.

Flavourings used before hops
Hay from the burned-out centre of the stack.

Bog myrtle, mugwort, wormwood, sweet gale, avens and rosemary.

Common clary
Some brewers of ale do put it into their drinke to make it more heady, fit to please drunkards.

Ground ivy was once the most commonly used, hence its other name, Ale-hoof.
It is good to tun up with new drink, for it will clarify it in a night, that it will be the fitter to be drank the next morning; or if any drink be thick with removing or any other accident, it will do the like in a few hours.

Yeast
No one ever bought yeast in country districts where everyone brewed. There was a 'yeast chain' where you borrowed from the person who had brewed last. This always ensured a good supply. The loan was repaid with beer later on.

Water
The water should be soft but not dead.

The wort of hard water does not ferment well.

Soft water brings the sweetness out of the malt and the bitterness out of the hops.

The best water is from springs, rivers, waterfalls and living wells.

Under-chalk water makes good beer.

The worst water is rainwater or peaty water and that from brackish and slow-running rivers.

Brewing terms

Although these are now mostly heard in breweries they were once in common use in every home, and if you make your own beer now they still apply.

liquor – any water used in the brewing process
mashing – mixing the malt and liquor
mash – the mixture of malt and liquor
wort – the liquid that is drained from the mash tub
sparging – washing the malt grains through with water after the wort has been drained off

Brewing utensils

Metal should be avoided as far as possible when brewing.

Keep utensils thoroughly clean and sterilize them before you start.

copper – this was essential to heat enough water.

brewing tub, mashing tub or keeper – for steeping and mashing the malt; made of wood, banded with metal with the top a little broader than the base and with a hole about 5 cm (2 in) wide in the bottom.

underbuck, underback or underdeck – a large wooden tub for the wort to run into when it is drawn from the grains.

filter – used when straining the wort from the mash. This can be in the form of a wilsh or wilch which fits over a tap on the inside of the tub like a sock; or a bundle of fine birch twigs. In the latter case, the hole was corked by a stick which had a weighted collar to hold down the birch.

tun-tub – for putting the beer in to work (this can also be done in the mashing tub).

horsehair sieve – for straining.

rack – on which to stand the sieve when straining (this could be a specially made frame or two stout, forked branches of a tree).

ladle and funnel – for pouring the beer into casks.

Brewing the beer

Get the malt thoroughly wet with cold water in the mashing tub. If this is not done, the water is spoiled.

Leave the malt for 15 minutes, covered with sacks to keep in the spirit of the malt.

Pour on the boiling liquor and stir for about 10 minutes to get a thick porridge.

Cover tightly and leave to stand for 4 hours.

Clear the filter and draw off the wort to the underbuck.

Sparge the malt that is left in the mash tub with hot water. You can now go on to add the hops to the wort or you can make a second wort with the used malt. This can be kept separate so you have a mild or small beer and a strong one, or the two can be mixed to make one beer of middling strength.

Put the wort into the copper and add the hops.

Boil for a long time (up to 4 hours) to get the most from the hops.

Turn off the copper and cool the wort so the hops sink to the bottom and form a filter bed.

Strain the wort through the hair sieve into the underbuck and sparge the hops with boiling water.

When the wort is 'milk warm' add the yeast.

Float one or two clean corks or a slice of toast on top of the wort so the yeast can collect round it as it begins to work.

When the yeast is working, the beer is 'on the smile' and can be left overnight.

The next morning, skim off the yeast into an earthenware bowl.

Bottling the beer

Make sure the bottles are clean and sterilized.

Add ½ teaspoon sugar to each 6 dl (1 pint) bottle of beer to make it ferment again and stay lively.

Putting the beer into casks

Cask sizes

pin – 41 litres (9 gallons)
firkin – 82 litres (18 gallons)
kil or kilderkin – 164 litres (36 gallons)

Make sure the casks are clean. Insert a chain in the bung-hole and roll the cask around to loosen any particles on the inside. Remove the chain and swill out the cask with boiling water.

Nettle juice seals cracks in leaking casks.

Transfer the beer to the cask using the ladle and funnel.

If the casks be not filled up, the beer will not be good, and certainly will not keep.

To preserve small beer without hops, mix a small quantity of treacle with a handful of wheat and bean flour and a little ginger; knead it and put it in the barrel.

The root of the yellow iris suspended in ale prevents it going sour.

Put the casks immediately to stand in a cool place and leave them undisturbed.

The cellar must be cool, of a good depth and dry.

For a quick and lively taste, put a handful of oatmeal into the barrel when it is first laid in the cellar.

Thunder is a spoiler of good malt liquor – counteract it by placing an iron bar across the cask, by fitting an iron pad over the bung-hole, or by putting an iron tray on top.

To recover ale or beer when it turns sour, put a handful of ground malt into the beer, stir it in and the beer will work and become good again.

Bad beer is 'sour as varges'. (Verjuice made from crab apples.)

Drinking the beer

Beer should not be drunk for at least a week after it is put into bottle or cask.

Drink your beer when it is good and do not give it the opportunity of going sour.

Too new is no profit, too stale is as bad,
Drink sower or dead maketh husband half mad.

After brewing, the household would invite the neighbours round to drink the new beer. They brought crusts of bread to dip into it for luck. This was called 'taking the shot'.

The best vessel for drinking beer is a pewter mug.

Keep tankards in the same place as the beer so they are the same temperature.

Ale! Ale! Glorious Ale!
Served up in pewter, it tells a fond tale.

Various names of beer
The Old October – the best of the October brew, very strong, usually saved for Christmas.
Key beer – another name for the strongest brew, so-called because it was kept under lock and key.
Spingo or Stingo – strong brews.
Huff-Cap or Hum-Cap – strong ales that would make you set your cap at a jaunty angle, or give you a humming in the head.
Table beer – fairly mild beer for all the family.
Tilly Willy – the mildest beer for the children.
Black Strap – a dark beer.
Dew beer – the beer bought with the shilling given to harvest workers by the farmer when the harvest contract was signed.
Trailing beer – bought from fines paid to the leader of the harvest workers by anyone who trampled standing-corn.

Bring us in good ale, and bring us in good ale!
For our blessed Lady's sake, bring us in good ale!

Country wines

Nature's yeasts are everywhere – country wines are man's improvement on her work.

Wine-making was not as essential as brewing in the country household, but it is an enjoyable occupation and its products add that certain spice to life. As with brewing, it was usually

done by Mother, and often by Grandmother who had more time and liked to make treats for her visiting family.
Wine can be made from flowers, herbs, berries, fruits and vegetables that grow in hedgerows and gardens. It can also be made with grains.

Flowers
(Omitting the rare or protected ones)
Dandelions
Broom or Gorse
Elderflowers (don't pick too many or you won't have any berries in the autumn).
Coltsfoot
Red clover
Marigolds
Old varieties of Roses

Herbs
Parsley
Balm

Wild berries and fruits
Rosehips
Hawthorn
Rowan berries
Elder
Blackberries
Whortleberry or blaeberry
Damsons
Sloes (most often used for sloe gin)
Crab apples

Fruits from the garden

Currants (red, black, white)
Strawberries
Raspberries
Gooseberries
Loganberries

Plums and greengages
Apples
Pears
Quinces
Rhubarb

Vegetables

Jerusalem artichokes
Potatoes
Parsnips
Beetroot
Carrots

Marrow
Celery
Spinach
Pea-pods
Nettles

Here the industrious huswives wend their way
Pulling the brittle branches careful down
And hawking loads of berrys to the town
Wi unpretending skill yet half divine
To press and make their eldern berry wine
That bottled up becomes a rousing charm
To kindle winters icy bosom warm
That wi its merry partner nut brown beer
Makes up the peasants christmass keeping cheer.

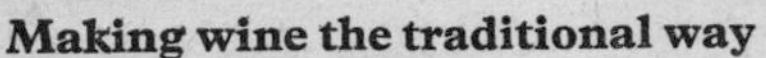

Making wine the traditional way

The two essential qualities that you must have to make good wine are cleanliness and patience.

The difference between natural and scientific wine-making is that in the latter all the natural yeasts are destroyed and tamed ones introduced.

Scientific wine-making is almost infallible – there is less risk but not so much pleasure and enjoyment.

Spontaneous fermentation gives a finer and more delicate wine, but there is more risk of the wine souring before the process starts.

When spontaneous fermentation is successful it gives the best results.

It is unnecessary to add nutrients such as epsom salts (magnesium sulphate), or tartaric acid and tannin – healthy fruit and vegetables contain everything needed in exactly the right proportions. (If you have an insipid fruit, add extra tannin by way of 1 cup of strong black tea per 4.5 litres (1 gallon). To increase tannin in cherry wine, leave a small piece of stem on each cherry.)

If any ingredient is not available, see what you can find to replace it – it may work even better.

Fruit should be at its peak of ripeness but still sound and wholesome.

The sooner you use the fruit after picking the better.

Hips, haws and rowan berries should be picked after the second hard frost.

Better wine can be made with good water.

Spring water is best for making wine, second is clear rainwater.

22 litres (5 gallons) is the ideal quantity to make at a time, but if you have a glut of fruit or not enough, make what comes and don't worry.

There are various ways of extracting the best from the fruit. You can boil it first but there is a danger of overboiling and the fruit could go too soft and make the wine cloudy.

If you choose the boiling method, do not use an aluminium or iron pan – it must be earthenware, copper or unchipped enamel (Aluminium and iron spoil the colour.)

To get the best flavour and ferment from the fruit, use the boiling water method:
Pulp the fruit well and pour on boiling water.

Fermenting on the pulp gives strength of flavour.

Never ferment wine in metal. Use an earthenware crock, a stone or glass jar, or best of all, wood.

Wood is porous enough for the wine to breathe but stout enough to keep out the vinegar bug.

A wooden cask gives a fine flavour and good colour.

Yeast works best at 19°–24°C (65°–75°F).

Don't overheat or overcool when the yeast is fermenting.

Once it is working well, unless it is in a very cold place, it should make enough heat of its own to continue.

The sediment in the bottom is called the 'mother of the wine'.

The vinegar bug, wine's most common enemy, lives in the air and waits for a chance to strike.
Keep him out by covering the fermenting vessel with a thick blanket or with several layers of old cotton curtains.

Once the vinegar bug is in, you can do nothing about it; but you have a good supply of wine vinegar.

The slower the process and the cooler the ferment, the finer the wine.

At first the yeast feeds on oxygen, later it needs to be fed with sugar.

Don't use too much sugar at a time. Add the first as it comes from the packet, and the rest, very gradually, in the form of syrup, tasting as you go.

Sugar brings up the alcohol content but there comes a time when the yeast stops working and all you are adding is sweetness.

By the addition of the right amount of sugar, the strongest wine can be either sweet, medium or dry.

The alcohol content of wine must be over ten per cent for it to keep. (With practice, you can bring it up to eighteen per cent.)

To clear wine, beat one egg white to a froth, beat it into 6 dl (1 pint) of wine and stir it into the cask. (This is enough for 91 litres (20 gallons).)

Bottle your wine when the trees from whence came the fruit are in bloom – then it will be light and sparkling.

Always sterilize wine bottles – wash them and put them into a hot oven for 15 minutes.

Always use new corks – old ones are never airtight.

Sterilize corks first by putting them into cold water and bringing them to the boil.

Seal the tops of bottles by dipping them in hot wax.

When the frost has stilled and cleared the standing water in the pond, it will have stilled and cleared the wine in the cellar.

Never open the wine before it is three months old.

Always set one bottle of each making aside and try it much late than the others. You will begin to learn the right age at which i should be opened.

Wines can be drunk straight from the bottle, but for the utmos clarity always decant naturally made country wines.

Old method for country wine
Pulp the fruit with a round-headed wooden beater. Tip it into wooden fermenting vessel or large earthenware crock. Add sugar. Pour on boiling water. Add the juice of 1 lemon. Spread baker's yeast on top of two pieces of toast and float them on to Cover with a blanket or old cotton curtains.
For the first few days, fermentation will be great, so skim off excess yeast every day. Do this until the yeast ceases to grow a it sinks to the bottom. Strain the wine into bottles and stand them on a tray. Set one bottle aside and, as the others froth ov keep topping them up from it. When all the frothing stops, co the bottles.

or
When the first fermentation has stopped, put the fermenting vessel into a warm place and feed gently with sugar syrup until the right point has been reached. Strain into bottles and cork.

6 A calendar of country recipes

Country food month by month

A man can't work with too much in his stomach, but he doesn't like to be hungry.

Everyday country food might seem simple, but it is tasty, warming and substantial and will see you well through any working day. It is inevitably seasonal as the recipes were devised long before the days of canning and freezing. There were specific times of the year for slaughtering animals when fresh meat was available and, very often, for the rest of the year there was only bacon or salt pork or beef.

Cheese was made mainly in the spring and summer and although there were hard cheeses enough to last through the winter, the lighter cream and curd cheeses and the other soft types that must be eaten fresh were available only when the sun shone and the cows were out to grass.

Vegetables obviously had their seasons and there were times when there were plenty of fresh ones around, and others when there were only dried beans and peas.

Salt meat (pork and bacon in particular) and cheese were two of the staples in the country diet. The others were beer and bread and other things made of wheat flour such as puddings, dumplings and fairly plain cakes made with lard and perhaps sweetened with currants. The flour was ground by the local miller and was much coarser and browner than the standard white flour of today. Often it was what we would now call wholemeal (with both the germ and the bran included), and the fine flour was similar to our 81% or 85% wholemeal flours with all the bran extracted but retaining the germ. If you want to get a fairly good representation of what country puddings and cakes tasted like then this would be the flour to use.

Often country food required long, slow cooking. This might seem very extravagant now in terms of fuel, but we must remember that in most cottages the open fire or kitchen range was burning all the time and the same amount of fuel was used whether the pot was placed over it or not. We may not have the time now to stand over a simmering pot and top it up occasionally or give it a loving stir, but cooking at one time worked into the other household chores when the housewife was at or near home all the time.

Interspersed with the ordinary working days were the highlights of the year. These were sometimes agricultural such as sheapshearing or harvest when all the helpers were fed from the farm kitchen during the work and a celebration was held when it was all over; or they were the religious festivals and feasts of Christmas and Easter which brought their own special treats. At any celebration the food was richer and full of spices. Sugar was fairly scarce and expensive, so plump, dried fruits and sometimes honey provided much of the sweetness.
This calendar of food concentrates mainly on the highlights of the year, but there are a few everyday ones as well.

January

What cheer? Good cheer, good cheer, good cheer!
Be merry and glad this good New Year.
Now Christmas is over, our Wassail begin,
Pray, open your door, and let us come in.

In many country districts the wassail bowl was carried round from house to house on New Year's Eve and also on Twelfth Night. The specially decorated bowl was made of maple or ash and was filled with 'lambswool' – hot spiced ale, thickened with egg yolks or cream, with brown toast and roasted apples floating on top. Sometimes the drink was carried round by the wassailers and given to the people in the houses in exchange for gifts of food or money, and sometimes it was provided by the people they visited in exchange for a song and New Year good wishes.

Wassail, wassail, all over the town,
The cup it is white and the ale it is brown;
The cup it is made of the good old ashen tree,
And so is the beer of the best barley.
We be good fellows, we drink to thee.

On New Year's Day special cakes were made in different districts. Triangular puff-pastry cakes, full of mincemeat, called Coventry God cakes were sold in the streets of Coventry, and Pope Lady cakes, made light and puffy with a large amount of egg white, in the streets of St Albans. In Aldburgh, Kitchel cakes were baked on New Year's Eve and were given as a present by godparents to their godchildren.

Pies were eaten all through the Christmas period and a special one was made for the final celebrations on Twelfth Night. The original version of this pie was found in an old recipe book written in the most delightful descriptive language. This is a modern adaptation. Serve it for any kind of buffet party. This should be enough for about 8 people.

A chicken pie for a festival occasion

0.9–1.3 kg (2–2½ lb) roasting chicken
350 g (¾ lb) lean ham cut from the bone
225 g (½ lb) best butcher's sausagemeat
sage and onion stuffing made with 25 g (1 oz) butter, 1 large onion
100 g (4 oz) wholemeal bread crumbs and 2 tablespoons chopped fresh sage
2 hardboiled eggs
salt and freshly ground black pepper
6 tablespoons chicken stock

pastry
650 g (1¼ lbs) plain 81% or 85% wholemeal flour
½ teaspoon salt
150 g (6 oz) lard
5 tablespoons milk
3 tablespoons water
beaten egg for glaze

Take the chicken off the bone and cut it into small pieces. Cut the ham into pieces the same size. Make the sausagemeat into small balls. Thinly slice the eggs. Soften the onion in the butter and work in the breadcrumbs and sage.
For the pastry, put the flour and salt into a mixing bowl. Warm the lard, milk and water in a saucepan until the lard melts and gradually beat them into the flour. Gather the dough into a ball and kneed it together on a floured board. Set aside enough to cover the top (about one-third) and roll out the rest. Line a large, high-sided dish (a soufflé or pâté dish) with the pastry (This kind of pastry is very difficult to handle so don't worry if it falls apart in places. Patch it up, making sure there are no gaps.)

Heat the oven to 180°C (350°F), Gas No. 4. Into the pastry lining put a layer of ham, chicken, sausagemeat and eggs. Spoon over some stuffing and season. Carry on until the dish is full. Pour in the stock. Cover the pie with the remaining pastry and decorate it with the trimmings. Brush with beaten egg and bake for 1½ hours.

Leave the pie in a cool place (not the refrigerator) overnight. 'Any cook who had suggested the Ice House for that poem of culinary perfection would have met with short shrift.'

(A cook who 'knew how to make the pie' came back year after year to see its due accomplishment. Her appearance at breakfast or lunch, with the cold pie, was greeted with cheers, and she retired with the half-crown which had been the mead of all perfect piemakers since 1834.)

Farewell words of Christmas:
Mark well my heavy doleful tale,
  For twelfth Day now is come,
And now I must no longer stay,
  And say no word but Mum.
For I, perforce, must take my leave
  Of all my dainty cheer –
Plum porridge, roast beef, and minced pies,
  My strong ale and my beer.

And so it was back to work again in the cold weather. Suet puddings are excellent food to keep out the cold, and this one could have been made from any bacon or ham left over from Christmas. It is part of childhood memories of Buckinghamshire.

Bacon and onion pudding

225 g ($\frac{1}{2}$ lb) 81% or 85% wholemeal flour
100 g (4 oz) suet (freshly grated if possible)
pinch salt
cold water to mix
1 medium-sized potato
350 g (12 oz) bacon pieces
225 g (8 oz) onions
6 chopped sage leaves
freshly ground black pepper

Put the flour, salt and suet into a bowl and mix them to a stiff dough with the water. Roll it out, reserving a piece for the top, and use it to line a pudding basin.
Scrub the potato (do not peel it) and dice it finely.
Finely chop the bacon and onion, mix them with the potato and sage and season with the pepper. Press the mixture into the pudding basin and cover the top with the reserved dough.
Cover with buttered greaseproof paper and a piece of foil (both with a large pleat in the middle), tie down and steam for 2$\frac{1}{2}$ hours.
Serve it with a green vegetable and brown gravy handed separately in a sauce boat. Serves 4.

February

Good morrow to you, Valentine;
Curl your locks as I do mine,
Two before and three behind,
Good morrow to you, Valentine.

Valentine buns, or plum shuttles were made on Valentine's Day in the county of Rutland. Made with a rich bread dough they are light and not oversweet. If you can get up early enough to make them on Valentine's Day serve them hot for breakfast with cream or butter. They are good cold, too, and you can have them with mid-morning coffee or with cheese for lunch or supper.

Valentine buns (or plum shuttles)

- 450 g (1 lb) wholemeal or 81% or 85% wholemeal flour
- 1 teaspoon salt
- 50 g (2 oz) lard or butter
- 25 g (1 oz) fresh or 15 g (½ oz) dried yeast
- 1 teaspoon sugar
- 1.25 dl (4 fl oz) milk
- 1.25 dl (4 fl oz) water
- 1 egg, beaten
- 100 g (4 oz) currants
- 1 tablespoon carraway seeds

Put the flour into a bowl with the salt and rub in the lard or butter. Cream the yeast with the sugar. Warm the milk and water to blood heat and mix them into the yeast. Put the mixture in a warm place for the yeast to froth. Make a well in the centre of the flour and pour in the yeast mixture and the beaten egg. Mix everything to a dough, turn it out on to a floured board and knead it well. Return it to the bowl, make a cross-cut in the top, cover it with a clean teacloth and leave it in a warm place for 1 hour to rise.

Heat the oven to 220°C (425°F), Gas No. 7. Knead the dough again and work in the currants and carraway seeds. Divide it into 16 pieces and form them into shuttle-shapes (long with a point either end). Lay them on a floured baking sheet, cover them with a cloth and stand them on top of the oven to prove for 10 minutes. Bake them for 20 minutes.

Shrovetide, the beginning of Lent, usually falls in February and, although the Church's strict rules about having to give up all meat (and sometimes dairy products as well) were relaxed considerably by the end of the Elizabethan era, the old tradition and some of the better Lenten foods have survived.

The two days before Lent begins are Collop Monday and Shrove Tuesday. On Collop Monday any joints of bacon that had been cut into but not finished were sliced into collops and fried with eggs. Any fresh meat was salted and hung up in the chimney to be ready in time for Easter. In Cornwall the day was known as Paisen Monday and it was the tradition there to eat pea soup.

Shrove Tuesday was, and still is, Pancake Day, when at one time all the butter, milk and eggs had to be used up. On some

farms the first pancake was thrown to the cockerel. If he ate it all himself the crops that year would be poor, but if he called the hens to share it the harvest would be plentiful.
Shroving songs were sometimes sung by children who went round asking for sweets and pancakes:

Shrove-tide is now at hand,
And we are come a-shroving;
Pray, dame, give us something,
An apple or a dumpling,
Or a piece of crumple cheese
Of your own making,
Or a piece of pancake.

Traditionally, pancakes should be served sprinkled with sugar and lemon juice, or spread with treacle, and rolled up.

Wigs and ale made a popular Lenten supper from the seventeenth century until the nineteen twenties. Wigs are light buns, made with eggs or milk, or both, and flavoured with spices and carraway seeds. Eaten warm straight from the oven, they are crisp on the outside and light as air in the middle. Serve them plain, with no butter, as they are rich enough. Or split them open and spread them with clear honey (again with no butter) so the honey melts into the bun.

Wigs

450 g (1 lb) 81% or 85% wholemeal flour
1 teaspoon salt
100 g (4 oz) butter
50 g (2 oz) plus 1 teaspoon soft brown sugar
2 teaspoons carraway seeds
25 g (1 oz) fresh or 15 g (½ oz) dried yeast
2.5 dl (8 fl oz) milk
4 tablespoons medium sherry or vintage cider

Rub the butter into the flour and mix in the salt, the 50 g (2 oz) sugar and the carraway seeds. Cream the yeast in a bowl with the teaspoon of sugar. Warm the milk to blood heat and mix it into the yeast. Leave in a warm place for 10 minutes to froth up. Make a well in the centre of the flour and pour in the yeast mixture together with the sherry or cider. Mix into a dough and

turn it out on to a floured board. Knead it well. Even at this stage it should feel light as air under your fingers. Return the dough to the bowl, make a cross-cut in the top, cover it with a cloth and put it in a warm place for 1 hour to rise.

Heat the oven to 200°C (400°F), Gas No. 6. Knead the dough again and roll it out to 2 cm ($\frac{3}{4}$ in) thick. Cut into triangle shapes and lay them on a floured baking sheet. Cover them with the cloth and set them on top of the oven for 20 minutes to prove. Bake them for 20 minutes so they are risen and golden brown.

Pudding pies were another sweet Lenten treat which were made mostly in Kent. You can eat them hot after the Sunday lunch or cold at teatime. The filling is rather like a creamy cheesecake with the currants or cherries at the botton to give you a sweet surprise.

Pudding pies

shortcrust pastry

150 g (6 oz) 81% or 85% wholemeal flour	100 g (4 oz) butter
pinch salt	water to mix

filling

40 g (1½ oz) ground rice
4.5 dl (¾ pint) milk
40 g (1½ oz) soft brown sugar
2 eggs, beaten
grated rind and juice 1 lemon
pinch grated nutmeg

for finishing

currants and chopped glacé cherries just to cover the bottoms of the tarts
little freshly grated nutmeg

Heat the oven to 180°C (350°F), Gas No. 4.
Make the pastry and set it aside to chill. Put the rice into a saucepan and gradually stir in the milk. Set it on a low heat and bring to the boil, stirring. Let the mixture simmer, uncovered, for 15 minutes, stirring occasionally. While it is cooking, roll out the pastry and line 24 patty pans, 2 small flan dishes or 4 small ovenproof dishes. Scatter currants on the bottom of half the pastry cases and the chopped cherries on the other half. When the rice is cooked, take the pan from the heat and beat in the butter, sugar, eggs and lemon rind and juice. Spoon the mixture on to the fruit, letting it come near the top of the pastry. Grate a little nutmeg over each one. Bake them in the centre of the oven for 1 hour. When they first come out they will be risen and golden brown, but they sink quite rapidly as they cool.

March

All the country is in an upturn, going out visiting. Girls and boys going home to see their mothers and taking them cakes.

The last Sundays of Lent
Tid-Mid, Misera.
Carlings, Palm and Pace-Egg Day.

Mid-Lent Sunday was originally when people went to visit their Mother Church and so it was called Mothering Sunday. Servants living away from home naturally had to return to do this and so they visited their parents at the same time. When the religious festival was forgotten, the mid-Lent tradition of home-visiting was continued. It had almost completely died out by the beginning of this century, but then, under American influence, Mothering Sunday was revived in the fifties, although it has come to have a slightly different connotation. The gift taken home to Mother was most frequently a simnel cake which was made by the children themselves or by the wife of their employer. It was accompanied by bunches of primroses and violets which they picked on the way.

I'll to thee a Simnel bring,
'Gainst thou go a-mothering;
So that when she blesseth thee,
Half that blessing thou'lt bring me.

Wholemeal simnel cake

225 g (8 oz) 85% wholemeal flour
large pinch salt
large pinch baking powder
50 g (2 oz) ground rice
225 g (8 oz) sultanas
100 g (4 oz) currants
100 g (4 oz) glacé cherries, halved
25 g (1 oz) chopped candied peel
225 g (8 oz) butter
grated rind 2 lemons
100 g (4 oz) soft brown sugar
4 eggs, separated
butter for greasing 20–cm (8–in) diameter cake tin

almond paste

225 g (8 oz) ground almonds
100 g (4 oz) soft brown sugar
1 egg, beaten
juice ½ lemon
1 tablespoon orange flower water
½ teaspoon almond essence

Heat the oven to 170°C (325°F), Gas No. 3. Mix the flour, salt, baking powder and ground rice together and set them aside. Weigh out all the fruit and peel and mix them together. Put the butter into a bowl, grate in the lemon rind and beat them together. Beat in the sugar and carry on beating until the mixture is light and fluffy. Beat in the egg yolks, one at a time. Stiffly whip the whites. Mix a quarter of them into the butter and then add a quarter of the flour. Do the same again and then mix in all the fruit. Then carry on with the rest of the whites and flour. Pile half the mixture into the cake tin and build it up slightly at the sides. Shape half the almond paste into a round, flat piece, smaller than the tin in diameter by about 4 cm (1½ in) and put it on top of the mixture smoothing it into the hollow. Finish with the remaining cake mixture and smooth the top. Bake the cake for 2 hours. Take it out and reset the oven to 190°C (375°F), Gas No. 5. Turn the cake out of the tin and set it on a floured baking sheet. Make the remaining almond paste into 8 small balls. Place them evenly round the top of the cake and flatten them so they are about 1 cm (½ in) thick. Put the cake back into the oven for 15 minutes. The paste will go a lovely golden brown and as it cools the top will harden and shine. Set the cake on a wire rack to cool.

Place it on a gold cakeboard (one of the covered cardboard ones) and tie it round with an orange- or peach-coloured ribbon.

To make the almond paste:
(This should be done before you make the cake.) Mix the almonds and sugar together. Beat the egg with the lemon juice, orange flower water and almond essence and then work it into the almonds and sugar. The mixture will be wet and sticky and not as manageable as ordinary marzipan, but the flavour and texture when it is cooked is far better.

Other Mothering Sunday food
Lamb with mint sauce, a well-boiled suet pudding, seakale, cauliflower, frumenty and homemade wine.
Roast veal, rice pudding and mince pies
Figgey pudding
Roast chine of pork

The lad and the lass on Mothering Day,
Hie home to their mother so dear,
'Tis a kiss for she and a kiss for they,
A chine of pork and a sprig of bay,
A song and a dance but never a tear.

Carlin or Carling Sunday was kept mainly in the north of England. Grey peas or dried beans were boiled until they were soft, mashed and fried in butter or bacon fat. They could be eaten as a savoury or sprinkled with sugar. If you cook them in bacon fat you can serve them on their own as a snack or have them with sausages or cold meats instead of potatoes.

Carlins

225 g (8 oz) pigeon peas
6 dl (1 pint) water
sea salt and freshly ground black pepper
100 g (4 oz) bacon pieces

Put the pigeon peas into a saucepan with the water, cover them, set them on a low heat and bring them to the boil. Turn off the heat and let the peas soak for 2 hours. Bring them to the boil again and simmer them for 2 hours (or until they are soft). Drain if necessary, mash them well (using a potato masher) and season with the salt and pepper.
Chop the bacon finely, put it into a frying pan and set it on a low heat until it is crisp and there is enough fat in the pan to cook the peas. Raise the heat to moderate, mix in the peas and fry them as you would mashed potatoes.

Figs were the traditional food all over the country on Palm Sunday. They were stewed and eaten with rice, put into a pie or made into a rich figgey pudding, similar to a Christmas pudding.

Figgey pudding

225 g (8 oz) dried figs
3 tablespoons sherry
50 g (2 oz) flour
50 g (2 oz) fresh brown breadcrumbs
50 g (2 oz) suet (freshly grated if possible)
1 teaspoon cinnamon
50 g (2 oz) soft brown sugar
grated rind and juice 1 lemon
1 egg, beaten
butter or lard for greasing small pudding basin

Finely chop the figs and soak them in the sherry for 2 hours. Put the flour, crumbs, suet and cinnamon into a bowl and work in the figs, sugar and lemon rind with your fingers. Make a well in the centre and add the sherry, lemon juice and beaten egg. Mix everything well and put into the prepared pudding basin. Cover with a layer of buttered greaseproof and foil (both with a pleat down the centre), tie down and steam for 3 hours. Serve it with custard or brandy butter. This should be enough for 4–6.

April

Good Friday comes this month: the old woman runs
With one a penny, two a penny 'hot cross buns'.
Whose virtue is, if you believe what's said,
They'll grow not mouldy like common bread.

Hot cross buns are derived from the small currant buns that were eaten during Lent in Elizabethan times. A cross was marked on the top as with all yeast breads to keep the Devil away and to help them to rise. Cromwell abolished all Lenten customs but, after the Restoration, the buns became symbolic and they have stayed with us ever since. It was thought that hot cross buns and any other bread baked on Good Friday would never go mouldy and one bun was kept back for the rest of the year and grated into water to cure digestive upsets in adults and children. In the towns, hot cross buns were made in the bakers' shops, but in the country they were always homemade.

Hot cross buns

450 g (1 lb) 81% or 85% wholemeal flour
½ teaspoon salt
1 teaspoon ground cinnamon
freshly grated nutmeg (about ½ a nut)
25 g (1 oz) fresh or 15 g (½ oz) dried yeast
1 tablespoon honey
3 dl (½ pint) milk
75 g (3 oz) butter
2 eggs, beaten
150 g (6 oz) currants
50 g (2 oz) chopped mixed peel

for making the crosses
shortcrust pastry made with 100 g (4 oz) 81 or 85% wholemeal flour and 50 g (2 oz) lard

for glaze
1 egg, beaten with 6 tablespoons water or milk

Put the flour into a mixing bowl with the salt and spices. Cream the yeast with the honey. Warm the milk to blood heat and mix it into the yeast. Put the mixture into a warm place for 10 minutes for the yeast to froth. Melt the butter in a saucepan on a low heat without letting it bubble. Make a well in the centre of the flour and pour in the yeast mixture, butter and eggs. Mix everything to a dough (it will be quite a sticky one!). Flour your hands well and turn the dough on to a floured board. Kneed it a little and then work in the currants and peel, one-third at a time. Return the dough to the bowl and make a deep cross-cut in the top. Cover it with a cloth and set it in a warm place for 1 hour to rise.

Heat the oven to 220°C (425°F), Gas No. 7. Make the pastry for the crosses. Knead the dough again and divide it into 16 round buns. Put them on a floured baking sheet with plenty of room in between. Roll out the pastry and cut it into thin strips. Lay them loosely over the tops of the buns to make the crosses Brush the buns and the crosses with the glaze and put them on top of the stove for 10 minutes to prove. Bake them for 20 minutes and cool them on a wire rack.

When Pasch (Easter) comes, grace comes,
Butter, milk and eggs.

Eggs symbolize rebirth. A broken egg provides food and the broken body of Christ spiritual food. So went the old teachings of the Church, and so every good Christian should eat eggs at Easter. More practically, chickens, ducks and geese start to lay prolifically at this time of the year and their eggs provide many a nourishing meal for the country household. One goose egg is all that you need for a tasty supper or lunch. Cook it with all the fresh herbs of spring.

Goose eggs baked with cheese and herbs

4 goose eggs
150 g (6 oz) grated cheddar cheese
1.5 dl (¼ pint) double cream
4 tablespoons chopped fresh spring herbs (parsley, thyme, savoury, marjoram and a little sage)

Heat the oven to 180°C (350°F), Gas No. 4.
Lightly grease a large, flat ovenproof dish. Put 100 g (4 oz) of the cheese evenly in the bottom. Break in the eggs, scatter the herbs and the rest of the cheese on top. Spoon the cream over the yolks. Bake the eggs for 20 minutes. Serves 4 as a supper dish.

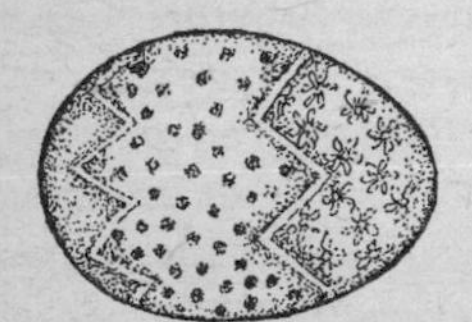

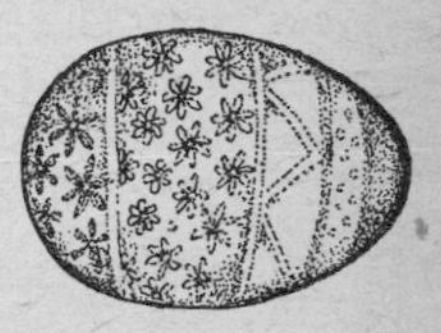

When Easter comes, who knows not then,
That veal and bacon is the man.

Easter has always been a celebration and the bacon would be brought down from where it had been smoking in the chimney, and the best roast meats would be cooked. What type of fresh meat you had varied according to your district. It could be lamb with mint or sorrel sauce, veal with sorrel sauce or pork stuffed with sage or ground ivy. The herbs served with the meats were supposed to represent the bitter herbs of Passover. Most of the old sorrel sauce recipes instruct you to blanch the sorrel first, but this rather spoils the taste and texture. The following method preserves it all. The sauce goes well with any joint of roast lamb or veal or with grilled chops.

Sorrel sauce for veal or lamb

50 g (2 oz) sorrel leaves
8 tablespoons red wine vinegar

Finely chop the sorrel. Put the vinegar into a small saucepan, set it on a low heat and bring it to the boil. Stir in sorrel and let it cook until it becomes dull green and soft (about 1½ minutes). Transfer it to a small sauceboat and serve it separately like mint sauce.

On Easter Sunday is the pudding seen,
To which the Tansy lends her sober green.

A tansy pudding was rather like a sweet omelette flavoured with tansy leaves and often served with apples. Tansy leaves were also sometimes put into Easter cakes.

Easter cakes were baked in many country districts on Easter Day. They are like rich, buttery biscuits and can be made with brandy and chopped peel, or with milk and no peel. They are crisp and light and excellent served with coffee or eaten as an accompaniment to a sweet mousse or junket. They will, if necessary, keep for up to a week in an airtight tin.

Easter cakes

225 g (8 oz) wholemeal flour
½ teaspoon ground cinnamon
½ teaspoon mixed spice
100 g (4 oz) butter
50 g (2 oz) currants
25 g (1 oz) chopped mixed peel
100 g (4 oz) soft brown sugar
juice ½ lemon
1 egg
1 tablespoon brandy

Heat the oven to 180°C (350°F), Gas No. 4.
Put the flour into a bowl with the spices and rub in the butter. Mix in the currants, peel and sugar with your hands. Make a well in the centre. Beat the lemon juice, egg and brandy together and pour them into the flour. Mix everything to a stiff dough and knead it lightly. Roll it out so it is 0·5 cm (¼ in) thick. Stamp it into rounds with a 6–7 cm (2½–3 in) biscuit cutter and lay them on a large, floured baking sheet. Bake them for 30 minutes and lay them on a wire rack to cool.

May

Hall-an-tow,
Jolly rumbelow,
We were up
Long before the day-o,
To welcome in the summer,
To welcome in the May-o!
Summer is a comin' in
And winter's gone away-o!

If you ever go out to watch the Morris dancers welcome the sun at five o'clock on May Day morning you are likely to be offered a piece of rich plum cake that is carried around spiked on a sword. It is the Morris man's communion.

The following recipe is rich and full of fruit and definitely improves on keeping. If you don't want it for May Day, it makes an excellent Christmas cake.

Rich plum cake

100 g (4 oz) butter
100 g (4 oz) soft brown sugar
2 eggs, beaten
225 g (8 oz) wholemeal flour
½ teaspoon bicarbonate of soda
1 teaspoon cinnamon
¼ nutmeg, grated
1.5 dl (¼ pint) cider
2 tablespoons brandy
150 g (6 oz) currants
150 g (6 oz) sultanas
150 g (6 oz) raisins
50 g (2 oz) chopped candied peel
butter papers for lining or butter for greasing a 17–cm (7–in) diameter cake tin

Heat the oven to 170°C (325°F), Gas No. 3.
Cream the butter and beat in the sugar. Gradually beat in the eggs. Mix the flour with the soda and spices and gradually beat it into the mixture alternately with the cider. Beat in the brandy. Fold in the fruit and peel. Put the mixture into the prepared cake tin and smooth the top. Bake the cake for 1¼ hours. Turn it out on to a wire rack to cool.

By the end of May the dairies would be in full production and the first cheeses would be just maturing. Double Gloucester cheese, made with the rich milk of Gloucester cattle, was often melted with beer and poured over bread for the evening meal.

Cheese and ale

225g (8 oz) farmhouse Double Gloucester cheese
2 teaspoons made English mustard
3 dl (½ pt) draught bitter
as much buttered brown toast as you need

Heat the oven to 200°C (400°F), Gas No. 6. Pare the cheese into small thin slivers with a sharp knife. Lay it in a heatproof dish and spread the mustard over the top. Pour in the beer and put the dish into the oven for 10 minutes. Spoon everything over the hot toast.

Curds and whey is easily made when there is plenty of fresh milk around. It isn't sweetened or flavoured like a junket and so it can be eaten as a cheap main meal. It is refreshing and creamy at the same time and seemingly more substantial than just drinking 3 dl (½ pint) of milk. (1 litre (2 pints) will make enough for four people.) Curds and whey, as well as making a quick and easy lunch, is excellent invalid food.

Curds and whey

1 litre (2 pints) milk
1 teaspoon junket rennet

Heat the milk to 30°C (86°F). Take the pan from the heat and stir in the rennet. Pour the mixture into a fairly deep dish, such as a pie dish and leave it in a cool place for 2 hours. Break up the curd to release the whey. Serve it plain with sweet or savoury biscuits, or sprinkle it with a little sugar or dried fruit.

Whitsun comes at the end of May and the traditional sweet on Whit Sunday is a tart made with the first gooseberries of the season. Make a plain tart and serve it with custard, or mix the two together to make a creamy filling.

Gooseberry custard tart

450 g (1 lb) gooseberries
2 elderflower sprigs
6 tablespoons white wine (or homemade gooseberry wine)
2 eggs, beaten
1.5 dl (¼ pint) double cream
4 tablespoons clear honey
shortcrust pastry to line 20-cm (8-in) diameter flan ring or pie plate

Heat the oven to 200°C (400°F), Gas No. 6.
Put the gooseberries into a saucepan with the elderflowers and wine. Cover them and set them on a low heat for 15 minutes, beating and stirring every so often so they cook to a pulp.
Rub them through a sieve and mix them with the eggs, cream and honey. Roll out the pastry and line the flan ring or pie plate. Pour the mixture into the pastry case and put the tart into the oven for 45 minutes. When it comes out, the top should be golden brown. Leave the pie until it is cool so it has a chance to set. It will be creamy and just slightly sharp.

Hit befell on Whitsuntide,
Early in a May mornyng,
The Sonne up fayre gan shyne,
And the briddis mery gan syng.

It was the custom in Cornwall to go walking in the country on Whit Sunday. The usual destination was a nearby farmhouse where the dairy was left open for parties of people to make Cornish Fuggan, or Heavycake. They took most of their own ingredients and the farmer provided the cream.

There are many recipes for heavy cake of varying degrees of

richness. Some are made with lard and sour milk, rather like scones or soda bread, and others contain clotted cream.

This one is the best of all. It isn't heavy-textured but light and rich at the same time, slightly crispy, and golden brown. It is best served hot and, if you are feeling extravagant, with more cream!

Cornish heavy cake

225 g (8 oz) clotted cream
225 g (8 oz) wholemeal flour
½ teaspoon salt
½ teaspoon bicarbonate of soda
75 g (3 oz) currants

Heat the oven to 200°C (400°F), Gas No. 6.
Put the cream into a mixing bowl. Mix the flour with the salt and soda and gradually beat it into the cream. When you have mixed nearly half with a spoon, knead the rest in with your hand, with the mixture still in the bowl. Knead in the currants in the same way. Form the dough into a round and roll it out so it is 2·5 cm (1 in) thick. Either place it on a floured baking sheet or lay it in a greased 17·5 cm (7-in) diameter skillet. Score the top into 12 or 16 triangles. Bake the cake for 1 hour. Serve it as hot as you can.

Then the Lord will send us a merry Whitsuntide!

June

In June comes the first main celebration in the farmer's year: Black Ram Night, or the sheepshearing supper.

Wife, make us a dinner, spare flesh neither corne,
Make wafers and cakes, for our sheep must be shorne.
At sheepe shearing neighbours none other thing crave,
But good cheer and welcome like neighbours to have.

Food at all the farming feasts was very similar. There were boiled salt pork and beef and sometimes roast pork, pies, pickles, cheese and plum puddings, and a barrel of strong ale, all supplied by the farmer.

To salt pork

1 kg (2 lb) joint belly of pork (streaky end)
1 tablespoon coarse salt
1 teaspoon saltpetre
2 bayleaves
10 juniper berries
10 allspice berries
1 tablespoon soft brown sugar

Mix the salt and saltpetre together. Crumble the bay leaves and crush the juniper and allspice berries together with a pestle and mortar. Mix these with the salt and sugar. Lay the pork (with the rind still on) in a flat earthenware or pyrex dish and rub the salt mixture into the surface. Cover it with a thick layer of greaseproof paper and put it into a cool place (not the refrigerator). Leave it for a week, turning it and rubbing the salt mixture into the surface every day. When you are ready to cook it, wash away all the brine and spices. Then boil it as you would a bought joint of salt pork.

Most meat pies were made with a raised pastry crust (like pork pie pastry). If you make it with the fat that has come from the meat filling the flavours of the inside and outside of the pie will be brought together.

Buy a shoulder of lamb, dice all the lean meat and render down all the fat as you would pork fat for lard (see under November). Clarify it, and use if for the pastry for mutton pies, which were a favourite at any feast. They make excellent picnic food or can be piled on the table for buffet parties.

Mutton pies

1 kg (2 lb) lean, boneless lamb cut from the shoulder
12 g ($\frac{1}{2}$ oz) mutton fat
2 medium onions, finely chopped
1 tablespoon chopped rosemary
salt and freshly ground black pepper

pastry

675 g ($1\frac{1}{2}$ lbs) 81% or 85% wholemeal flour
1 teaspoon salt
175 g (6 oz) clarified mutton fat
9 tablespoons water

glaze

1 egg beaten with 2 tablespoons double cream

Heat the oven to 170°C (325°F), Gas No. 3.
The pastry is best used as soon as it is made, so prepare the filling first. Cut the meat into 1-cm (½-in) pieces and put it into a mixing bowl. Melt the fat in a frying pan over a low heat, mix in the onions and cook them until they are transparent and just beginning to soften. Mix them into the lamb with the rosemary and season well.

For the pastry, put the fat and water into a small saucepan and set it on a low heat for the fat to melt. Mix quickly into the flour and salt and knead everything to a smooth dough. Use the pastry to line 12 individual soufflé dishes or ramekins, saving enough for the tops. Fill the pastry cases with the lamb mixture, pressing it down firmly to get as much in as possible, as it shrinks while cooking. Cover the tops and seal the edges inside the outer rim of the dishes (this ensures easy turning-out). Brush the tops with the egg and cream and bake the pies for 1½ hours. Let them stand for 10 minutes after coming out of the oven, then turn them out and stand them on a wire rack to cool.

Cheese cakes and curd tarts have been a favourite country sweet for many years and were often served at the farming feasts.

Curd tart

pastry to line a 17.5-cm (7-in) diameter pie plate:

100 g (4 oz) wholemeal flour
50 g (2 oz) butter
pinch salt
cold water to mix

filling

225 g (8 oz) curd cheese
50 g (2 oz) soft brown sugar
2 eggs, beaten
50 g (2 oz) currants

Make the pastry and set it aside to chill. Heat the oven to 200°C (400°F), Gas No. 6. Cream the cheese in a bowl and beat in the sugar. Add the eggs, a little at a time and fold in the currants. Roll out the pastry and line the pie plate. Fill it with the cheese mixture and smooth the top. Bake the tart for 40 minutes, or until the top is golden brown and well risen. Let it cool completely before you eat it. (When the tart comes out of the oven the filling will be risen high above the sides, but as it cools, it sinks back down again and the top becomes smooth and glossy.)

Now the sheep are all shorn and the wool carried home
Here's a health to our master and flock,
And if we should stay till the last goes away,
I'm afraid 'twould be past twelve o'clock.

July

Between haymaking and harvest is the farmer's holiday time when there are fairs and agricultural shows.
Sweetmeats and little cakes were sold by stallholders and one of the most popular was gingerbread. It was made in all shapes and sizes. There were hunting nuts which were quite small, oval and convenient for putting in your pocket, and larger gingerbreadmen with their currant faces and buttons.

Gingerbreadmen

225 g (8 oz) 81% or 85% wholemeal flour
pinch salt
½ teaspoon bicarbonate of soda
2 teaspoons ground ginger
50 g (2 oz) butter
50 g (2 oz) lard
100 g (4 oz) golden syrup
100 g (4 oz) sugar
currants for eyes, nose and buttons
lard for greasing baking sheet
gingerbreadman mould

Heat the oven to 180°C (350°F), Gas No. 4. Put the flour, salt, soda and ginger into a bowl. Put the butter, lard, syrup and sugar into a saucepan and set them on a low heat so they all melt together. Make a well in the centre of the flour and stir in the contents of the saucepan to make a stiff cake mixture. Grease a large baking sheet with lard. Lay your mould on one corner of the sheet (but not right on the edges) and fill it with the mixture to about 1 cm (⅜ in) thick. Carefully take away the mould and lay it further along, leaving a gap between the two to allow for spreading during cooking. Carry on until all the mixture is used up (you should make about 6 men). Make eyes, nose and buttons with currants and bake the gingerbreadmen

for 20 minutes. Cut them apart if they are holding hands and lift them on to a wire rack to cool. (They may be a little soft when you take them out, but they will harden as they cool.)

Broody hens were encouraged to sit at the beginning of the summer and by July the young chickens would be plump enough for the pot. Chicken pie is a country favourite and there were ways of making it in summer and ways for winter. With parsley and flaky pastry a chicken pie is light and summery.

Chicken and parsley pie

1.3–1.6 kg (3–3½ lb) roasting chicken
25 g (1 oz) chopped parsley
grated rind 1 lemon
salt and freshly ground black pepper
¼ teaspoon ground mace
2 tablespoons wholemeal flour
2 tablespoons melted chicken fat or butter
1 medium onion, thinly sliced
3 dl (½ pint) chicken stock (made from the bones or giblets)
flaky pastry made with 175 g (6 oz) 81% or 85% wholemeal flour
beaten egg for glaze

Joint and bone the chicken. Remove the coarser skin. Chop the meat into small pieces. Put it into a bowl and mix in the parsley, lemon rind, seasonings, mace and flour. Heat the fat or butter in a frying pan on a low heat, mix in the onion and let it soften. Cool it a little and mix it into the chicken. Heat the oven to

200°C (400°F), Gas No.6. Put the chicken filling into a large pie dish and put a pie funnel in the middle. Cover the pie with the pastry and brush the top with beaten egg. Decorate round the funnel with any trimmings and brush with egg again. Bake the pie for 1 hour.

August

Beneath some shelt'ring heap of yellow corn
Rests the hoop'd keg and friendly cooling horn.

The harvest begins in August and at one time every available person went out into the fields to help. Lunch baskets were packed up and stone jars of cider and small beer were put under hedges and amongst the cut sheaves to keep cool.

To keep you going through the day there was bread and cheese, bacon, wigs, apple pies and pasties, and pies made from meat and potato left over from the previous night's supper. Pancakes were sometimes used instead of pastry to wrap up the meat for taking out into the fields.

The following recipe (including the title) is based on one from the same book as the festive pie. It makes ideal picnic food and is delicious plain or with cheese. Add the spices and it can be eaten as a sweet.

A biscuit - a plain cake for putting in a man's dinner basket

450 g (1 lb) wholemeal flour
2 teaspoons baking powder
50 g (2 oz) lard or dripping
100–175 g (4–6 oz) currants
3 dl (½ pint) skimmed milk
lard to grease

2 17.5–cm (7–in) diameter skillets or cake tins
optional spices:
a little nutmeg,
cinnamon or mixed spice

Heat the oven to 200°C (400°F), Gas No. 6. Put the flour and baking powder into a bowl and rub in the lard or dripping.

Toss in the currants (and spices if you are using them) with your fingertips. Mix in the skimmed milk to make stiff dough. Divide it into two and press each piece into a greased tin or skillet. Score the top of each into 12 wedges. Bake the cakes for 30 minutes and cool them on a wire rack. Cut them into wedges and cart them off on a picnic.

In the evening, the harvest workers were fed from the farm kitchen. There would be salt pork with broad beans, or salt beef with carrots, turnips, cabbage and potatoes. Very often these boiled meats were accompanied by a plum pudding, which could be simply made with flour, suet and water, or richer with milk and eggs. Currants or raisins were always added. This one is of the richer kind. It goes surprisingly well with meat and brown gravy, and if there is any left over you can eat it with melted honey or syrup.

A rich plum pudding

225 g (8 oz) 81% or 85% wholemeal flour
½ teaspoon salt
100 g (4 oz) freshly grated suet
100 g (4 oz) raisins
2 eggs, beaten
8 tablespoons milk
little butter or lard for greasing basin, and greaseproof paper

Mix the flour, salt, suet and raisins in a bowl. Make a well in the centre and mix in the eggs and milk. Work everything to a dough (it will be quite a moist one) and put the mixture into a greased pudding basin. Put a piece of greased greaseproof paper and a piece of foil over the top (both with a large pleat in the middle) and tie down. Steam the pudding for 3 hours. Turn it out on to a plate and take it to the table with a knife so everyone can help themselves to as much as they want.

Rabbits were often shot in the harvest fields for the evening's supper. To make a small rabbit into a substantial meal, boil it in a pudding.

Rabbit pudding

1 wild rabbit, giving about 450 g (1 lb) meat
100 g (4 oz) bacon pieces
1 large onion
2 medium-sized cooking apples
1 tablespoon dried sage
75 ml ($\frac{1}{8}$ pint) dry cider
freshly ground black pepper
225 g (8 oz) wholemeal flour
100 g (4 oz) freshly grated suet
pinch salt
1 tablespoon chopped parsley
cold water to mix
lard for greasing
9 dl ($1\frac{1}{2}$ pint) pudding basin

Take all the rabbit meat from the bones and chop it into small pieces. Dice the bacon, slice the onion, and peel, quarter, core and chop the apples. Mix them with the rabbit, sage and pepper. Put the flour into a bowl with the suet, salt and parsley and make it into a stiff dough with the water. Reserve enough for the top, roll out the rest and line the greased basin. Fill the pudding with the rabbit mixture, cover the top and seal the edges. Cover the pudding with a layer of greased greaseproof paper and foil (with a 2·5-cm (1-in) pleat in the centre). Tie it down and steam the pudding for 2 hours.

In some districts the main meal of the day was eaten at noon. In this case, supper was simple but very sustaining. It could have been a possett. This is basically a dish of breadcrumbs with hot milk and beer or wine poured over them so the milk curdles. Sugar and sometimes spices were added and for special occasions the dish was enriched with ground almonds. This one is a simple worker's possett. It would be ideal for breakfast, or for lunch when you come in from the cold.

Worker's possett

350 g (12 oz) breadcrumbs (or crumbs from a rich teabread such as wigs or Sally Lunn)
4 tablespoons soft brown sugar
6 dl (1 pint) milk
6 dl (1 pint) stale draught bitter

Divide the bread between four large bowls and add the sugar. Heat the milk to boiling point and pour it over the bread. Warm the beer and pour it into the milk. Serve straight away.

September

Then comes the harvest supper night
Which rustics welcome with delight.

All the best food was saved for the harvest supper. There were usually cold meats – pork, salt beef, chicken, goose and sometimes hare, raised pies and plum puddings. The summer's cheeses would be mature and there would be plenty of apples and perhaps a pumpkin for spiced, sweet pies. As well as this there were custards and junkets, cream, figgey puddings, tarts and ginger cakes. And always a barrel of strong ale or vintage cider or perhaps both.

Salted brisket can be made fairly cheaply and is excellent for any cold table at parties or at Christmas.

Salt beef in old ale

1.8 (4 lb) piece of brisket, unrolled and weighed after boning
50 g (2 oz) coarse salt
1 teaspoon saltpetre
3 bayleaves
$\frac{1}{2}$ teaspoon ground mace
12 allspice berries
12 black peppercorns
1 clove garlic
2 tablespoons soft brown sugar

Put the salt and saltpetre together in a bowl, crumble in the bayleaves and add the mace. Crush the allspice, pepper and garlic together and add them to the salt with the sugar. Lay the beef in a large, flat earthenware or pyrex dish and rub the salt mixture well into the surface. Cover it with a thick layer of greaseproof paper and leave it in a cool place for a week, turning it and rubbing the brine into the surface every day. At the end of the week, take it out and wash it.

For boiling you will need
6 dl (1 pt) old ale (specially brewed by independent brewers at Christmas)
water to cover completely
1 teaspoon cloves
1 teaspoon black peppercorns
1 small onion, cut in half but not peeled
1 stick celery broken into several pieces
1 small carrot, cut in half lengthways

Put the beef into a saucepan with the boiling ingredients. Bring it to the boil, skim, cover and simmer for 1½ hours. Take out the beef and let it cool completely overnight (not in the refrigerator).

Raised pies were made with pork, game and rabbit. This one is moist and meaty with crispy pastry, and looks superb cut into slices.

Raised rabbit pie with prunes

1 wild rabbit
4 rashers unsmoked streaky bacon
12 g (½ oz) pork dripping or lard
1 medium onion, finely chopped
1 tablespoon chopped thyme
sea salt and freshly ground black pepper
6 prunes, soaked overnight in cold water

pastry

350 g (12 oz) wholemeal flour
½ teaspoon salt
freshly ground black pepper
75 g (3 oz) lard
6 tablespoons water
one 1–kg (2–lb) loaf tin
beaten egg for glaze

Dice all the rabbit meat. Blanch the bacon rashers by bringing them to the boil. Drain them and refresh them with cold water. Chop them and put them into a bowl with the rabbit. Melt the dripping or lard in a small frying pan on a low heat. Mix in the onion and let it soften. Mix it into the rabbit with the thyme and seasonings.

Heat the oven to 170°C (325°F), Gas No. 3. Put the flour, salt and pepper into a bowl. Put the lard and water into a saucepan and set them on a low heat until the lard has melted. Stir them quickly into the flour and knead everything to a dough. Set aside one-third to make the top of the pie and use the rest to line the loaf tin. Put in half the filling. Stone the prunes and lay them in a line along the centre of the pie. Put in the rest of the filling. Cover the top with the remaining pastry and seal the edges inside the rim of the tin. Brush with beaten egg. Make a small round hole in the centre of the pastry, decorate round it with trimmings and brush with egg again. Bake the pie for 2 hours. Let it rest in the tin for 30 minutes and then turn it out on to a wire rack to cool. Leave it overnight in a cool place.

Seed cake was eaten all the way through the harvest and often appeared at the harvest supper table. Carraway seeds were thought to give the workers strength. They were also thought to prevent stealing and giving it to the men could have been a way of binding loyalty to the farm.

Seed cakes could be like sponge cakes, but more often they were made with yeast like a rich bread. This one is moist and sweet and should really be eaten without butter.

Seed cake

12 g (½ oz) fresh or dried yeast
1 teaspoon sugar
2 tablespoons warm water
225 g (8 oz) wholemeal flour
pinch salt
1 tablespoon carraway seeds
50 g (2 oz) butter
50 g (2 oz) sugar
1 egg beaten and made up to 1·5 dl (¼ pint) with sherry or vintage cider.

Cream the yeast with the sugar and water and put it in a warm place to froth. Put the flour into a bowl with the salt and carraway seeds and rub in the butter and sugar. Make a well in the centre and pour in the frothed yeast, egg and sherry. Mix everything to a dough, turn it on to a floured board and knead it well. Return it to the bowl, make a cross-cut in the top, cover it with a cloth and put it in a warm place for 1 hour to rise. Heat the oven to 200°C (400°F), Gas No. 6. Grease a 12·5-cm (5-in) diameter cake tin (with high sides). Knead the dough again and punch it down into the tin. Cover it with a cloth and set it on top of the stove for 20 minutes to prove. Bake the cake for 45 minutes. Turn it on to a wire rack to cool.

There were celebrations in the hop gardens, too, when all the hops had been gathered in and dried. In Kent, the supper was called a hopkin (the harvest supper was a wheatkin) and it was held either in the oast house or in the farm kitchen. Oast cakes are like a cross between crispy pancakes and lardy cakes.

Oastcakes to eat at a hopkin

450 g (1 lb) 81% or 85% wholemeal flour
50 g (2 oz) lard
pinch salt
1 teaspoon baking powder
100 g (4 oz) currants
a nice drop of parsnip wine
1.5 dl (¼ pint) water
lard for frying

Put the flour into a bowl and rub in the lard, salt and baking powder. Mix in the currants. Make a well in the centre and mix in the wine and water so you have a very moist dough. Melt enough lard in a frying pan on a moderate heat to give you ·5 cm (¼ in) of fat. Take 1 tablespoon of the dough, put it into the pan and spread it out to a flat round cake (it's almost impossible to get even-shaped rounds – they're all very irregular) about ·5 cm (¼ in) thick. Put in another spoonful of dough and do the same. Fry them until they are golden brown on both sides. Remove them and keep them warm. Carry on cooking until all the dough is used up, adding more lard as you need it. 'Don't hang about, but set down and eat 'em, hot's hot!'

Here's a health to our master, the founder of the feast,
I hope to God in Heaven his soul may be at rest;
That all things may prosper whatever he takes in hand,
For we are all his servants and all at his command.
So drink, boys, drink, and see you do not spill,
For if you do you shall drink two,
It is our master's will.
(Toast at the harvest supper)

October

By October, the new wheat is dry, threshing has started and there will be plenty of flour for bread, dumplings and cakes. The basic recipe for household bread has remained the same for centuries.

Household bread

1.3 kg (3 lbs) wholemeal flour plus extra for kneading
2 tablespoons salt
50 g (2 oz) fresh yeast (or 1 oz dried)
2 teaspoons sugar or honey
9 dl (1½ pints) whey, buttermilk or water warmed to blood heat
lard for greasing tins or pots, or flour for coating baking sheets

Put the flour and salt into a bowl. Cream the yeast with the sugar or honey and 3 dl (½ pint) of the liquid. Stand it in a warm place to froth. Make a well in the centre of the flour and pour in the yeast mixture and the remaining liquid. Mix everything to a dough, turn it out on to a floured board and knead it well. Return the dough to the bowl, make a cross-cut in the top, cover it with a cloth and set it in a warm place for 1 hour to rise. Heat the oven to 200°C (400°F), Gas No. 6. Knead the bread again and divide and shape it as you wish. Cover the loaves with a cloth and put them on top of the stove for 20 minutes to prove. Bake the small loaves for 40 minutes and the large ones for 50 minutes. Turn the bread on to a wire rack to cool and leave it for 12 hours.

Cooking apples are big and mellow in October so use the new wheat to make apple dumplings or a large apple pudding. This one, based on an eighteenth-century recipe, is made with a crust similar to that used for raised pies which makes it very substantial. It was probably served with custard or with cream as the main evening meal when there was nothing with which to make a savoury or meat dish. Serve it alone for high tea or after a very light salad meal. It is really delicious but far too much after a large dinner.

Apple pudding

filling

2 large Bramley apples
75 g (3 oz) soft brown sugar
½ teaspoon ground cinnamon
4 whole cloves

crust

225 g (8 oz) 81% or 85% wholemeal flour
pinch salt
½ teaspoon bicarbonate of soda
1.5 dl (¼ pint) milk
50 g (2 oz) lard

Peel, core and chop the apples. Put them in a bowl and mix in the sugar, cinnamon and cloves and leave them while you make the crust. Put the flour, salt and soda into a bowl and make a well in the centre. Put the milk and lard into a saucepan and set them on a low heat until the lard has melted. Pour them into the flour and mix everything to a dough. Take aside one-third to make the top, roll out the rest and use it to line a greased pudding basin. Fill it with the apple mixture, pressing it down hard if it looks as if it will be a tight fit. Cover it with the remaining pastry and seal the edges. Cover with a layer of buttered greaseproof and foil (with a pleat down the centre), tie down and steam the pudding for 2½ hours. Turn it out on to a fairly high-sided dish so the juices don't run away when you cut it. Serve the pudding with homemade custard or cream.

The main cereal in the North of England was oats. There would be oatmeal bread and porridge and crispy oatcakes which were cooked on a girdle over the fire. They are superb with cheese and keep well in an airtight tin.

Oakcakes

To make 24

225 g (½ lb) fine or medium oatmeal plus a little extra for kneading
½ teaspoon salt
½ teaspoon bicarbonate of soda
18 g (¾ oz) lard
1.5 dl (¼ pint) water

Put the oatmeal, salt and soda into a bowl. Put the lard and water into a saucepan and set them on a low heat until the lard has melted. Stir them quickly into the oatmeal to make a stiff dough. Turn it on to a board and knead it lightly. Divide it into two and roll each piece into a round about ·5 cm (¼ in) thick. Cut each one into 12 triangles. Heat a girdle on a low heat with no fat and heat the grill to moderate. Lay as many triangles as possible on the girdle and as soon as their edges begin to curl and the undersides just begin to brown, transfer them to the grill. Cook them until the top is slightly brown, being careful not to burn them. Lay them on a wire rack to cool.

October is the pickling month when any remaining summer vegetables were preserved for use during the winter. In the fields at the beginning of the month should be small, white button mushrooms which made one of the most favourite pickles.

Pickled mushrooms

225 g (8 oz) small button mushrooms
2 teaspoons salt
¼ teaspoon cayenne pepper
3 dl (½ pint) white wine or white malt vinegar
6 allspice berries
6 cloves
6 black peppercorns
2 blades mace

Sprinkle the mushrooms with the salt and let them stand for 4 hours. Drain and dry them. Put them into an enamel saucepan and sprinkle them with the cayenne pepper. Set the pan on a very low heat. Put the spices and vinegar into another saucepan, cover them, bring them to the boil and simmer for 10 minutes. Strain the vinegar and discard the spices. The liquid should now be running from the mushrooms. Pour the vinegar over them, let it boil up and immediately take the pan from the heat. Let the mushrooms cool and put them with

their liquid into a screwtopped jar. Keep them for at least 2 days before using them – the longer the better.

November

At Hallontide (11 November), slaughter-time entereth in,
And then doth the husbandman's feasting begin:
From thence unto Shrovetide kill now and then some,
Their offal for household the better will come.

The animals that had been growing fat all summer were slaughtered in November and thereafter throughout the winter, so there was fresh meat and meat for salting.

The fat from the pigs was used to make lard, and if you can buy enough pork fat (it is sold in some supermarkets) it is well worth making your own now, not so much in terms of cost but for flavour and quality.

Lard

450–550 g (1–1½ lb) pork fat (preferably from the belly but it isn't essential)

Remove any tough pieces of skin from the fat and then chop it into 1-cm (½-in) dice. Put into a heavy saucepan, cover it and set it on a low heat. Leave them for about 15 minutes so there will be plenty of liquid fat inside the pan and the fat pieces are golden brown but not burnt. If possible, turn the pieces halfway through, but be careful or the fat will splatter dangerously. Take the pan from the heat and leave it for about 15 seconds. Then carefully lift the lid, standing back a little. Turn the fat, replace the lid and put the pan back on the heat. Strain the fat through a metal sieve into a bowl or dripping cups, pressing down hard on the fat. Save the fat pieces (see below).

The fat you have now – about 3–4 dl (½–¾ pint) – is excellent for all kinds of frying, sweating vegetables, and browning meat before casseroling. It is also good for shortcrust pastry for savoury pies. If you want to make a sweet cake with lard, or for raised pie pastry, it is best to clarify the fat. Put the fat into a saucepan with twice its amount of water. Cover the pan, bring the contents slowly to the boil and simmer them for 2 minutes. Strain the liquid through muslin or absorbent kitchen paper and leave it to cool completely. The clarified fat will set on the top so you can skim it off in white, creamy lumps.

Even the tiny pieces of golden fat were not wasted, but used to make cakes. The method throughout the country was the same but the name varied. Amongst other things, the cakes were called browsels, crinkling, scrap and scran cakes.

This recipe makes a rich brown-coloured cake, deliciously spicy, in which the pieces of fat have not quite melted but don't taste like pork. It might sound peculiar now, but it is quite delicious.

Crinkling cake

100 g (4 oz) fat pieces made from rendering down about 650 g (1½ lb) fat (don't worry if it is a fraction over or under)
225 g (8 oz) wholemeal flour
1 teaspoon baking powder
1 teaspoon ground cinnamon
1 teaspoon mixed spice
100 g (4 oz) Barbados sugar
1 egg, beaten
1.5 dl (¼ pint) milk
lard to grease 20-cm (8-in) diameter cake tin

Heat the oven to 170°C (325°F), Gas No. 3.
Mix the fat, flour, baking powder, spices and sugar in a mixing bowl. Make a well in the centre and mix in the egg and milk. Pile the mixture into the prepared cake tin and smooth the top. Bake the cake for 1 hour. Turn it on to a wire rack to cool.

The lard itself can be used instead of butter in cake mixtures, or you can save a piece of bread dough to make lardy (or fatty) cake. You can pull it apart in rich, sugary layers and although it is only made of dough it seems to melt in your mouth. It is best eaten still slightly warm, or at least on the day that you cook it.

Lardy cake

When you are making your household bread, set aside a portion made with 225g (8 oz) flour to make the cake

You will also need

175 g (6 oz) lard
½ teaspoon ground cinnamon
freshly grated nutmeg
50 g (2 oz) granulated or demerara sugar
25 g (1 oz) currants
25 g (1 oz) sultanas
lard for greasing tin

Heat the oven to 200°C (400°F), Gas No. 6 (as for bread). After the dough has been kneaded with the rest for the second time, roll it out to an oblong. Spread 25 g (1 oz) of the lard on two-thirds of it and fold it into three. Roll it out again and spread on a quarter of the lard that is left. Sprinkle it with a quarter of the spices, sugar and fruit. Repeat this three times. The last time you fold the dough, do not roll it again but leave it as it is and lay it in a greased roasting tin or Swiss roll tin. (If you lay it on a baking sheet the melting lard will run all over the oven.) Put the tin on top of the stove, cover the cake with a cloth and let it prove for 15 minutes. Bake it for 40 minutes. Transfer it to a wire rack for 10 minutes to cool a little and eat it as soon as you can.

December

Welcome Christmas which brings us all good cheer,
Pies and puddings, roast pork and strong beer.

Preparations for Christmas really began at the end of November when all the puddings, cakes and mincemeat were made, the poultry looked over and fattened up, and the other animals killed.

Brawn and soused meat were once as essential in the Christmas feast as turkey is today. Brawn was not just made with the head and trotters, but with all the foreparts of the pig so it was rich and meaty. This festive brawn, made in a similar way, but on a smaller scale, is ideal for supper on Christmas night.

Festive brawn

2 knuckle joints ham, soaked overnight
2 meaty trotters
2 pigs' tongues
900 g (2 lb) lean pork (shoulder joints are good)
2 medium onions, cut in half but not peeled
2 carrots, cut in half lengthways
2 sticks celery, broken into piec
10 peppercorns
10 allspice berries
10 cloves
2 blades mace
2 bay leaves
6 dl (1 pint) dry cider
extra water to cover

Put the meat and vegetables into a large saucepan with the spices and bayleaves. Pour in the cider and top up with water. Bring them slowly to the boil and skim. Simmer for 1½ hours. Remove all the meat and strain the stock through muslin. Return the stock to the rinsed-out pan and let it boil while you chop the meat. Remove all the gristle and rind from the meat and as much or as little fat as you like. Chop what is left into dice. Put it into an earthenware dish or mould and press down hard. Cool the stock a little and pour enough into the dish to only just cover the meat. Put the brawn into a cold place to set.

Meat was often put into a 'sousing drink' to preserve it. This was sometimes just a salt-and-water brine with herbs, but for special occasions it would contain wine, beer or cider. Again, here is a small scale recipe suitable for a modern Christmas party.

Soused pork shoulder

1 piece rolled shoulder of pork weighing about 1 kg (2–2½lb)
1 litre (2 pints) dry cider
1.5 dl (¼ pint) cider vinegar
1 small onion, roughly chopped but not peeled
1 medium carrot, roughly chopped
1 stick celery, roughly chopped
few celery leaves
2 teaspoons black peppercorns
2 teaspoons cloves
2 bayleaves
large bouquet garni
1 large cooking apple

Keep the pork in one piece and put it into a large non-corrosiv container (earthenware, plastic or pyrex). Put all the rest of th ingredients into a saucepan and bring them gently to the boil.

Let them simmer for 10 minutes, cool them and pour them over the pork. Cover the container with a flat piece of wood or, if it has a plastic fitting lid, leave a breathing gap. Leave the pork in the sousing drink for 3 days. Take the pork from the 'drink', wash it and pat it dry with kitchen paper. Put it into a casserole. Heat the oven to 170°C (325°F), Gas No. 3. Roughly chop the apple without peeling or coring and put it round the pork. Cover the casserole and put it into the oven for 2 hours. Lift out the pork and put it on an ovenproof dish. Turn the oven up to 200°C (400°F), Gas No. 6. Put the pork into the oven for 10 minutes to just crisp the outside. Remove it and let it cool completely. Cut it in slices to serve.

The traditional accompaniment to brawn and souse was a creamy mustard sauce made with flour and milk and served from a jug.

Mustard sauce for brawn and souse

25 g (1 oz) butter
1 tablespoon wholemeal flour
1 tablespoon mustard powder
4.5 dl (¾ pint) milk

Melt the butter in a saucepan over a moderate heat. Stir in the flour and mustard powder and cook them, stirring, for 1 minute. Take the pan from the heat and stir in the milk. Replace the pan and bring the sauce to the boil, stirring. Simmer for 1 minute. Pour the sauce into a jug and cover the surface with wet greaseproof paper. Leave the sauce in a cool place until it is cold. You should be able to pour it from the jug on to your meat.

On Christmas Eve, the Old October or other strong ale was tapped, the cider brought in from the orchard, and the sloe gin or cherry brandy opened. Elderberry wine was mulled for a warming nightcap and for supper there were mince pies, yule or peppercake (in Yorkshire) and cheese.

On Christmas morning there was frumenty (furmety or furmenty – there are may variations) for breakfast. This was wheat, gently steeped in a low oven until it was soft and

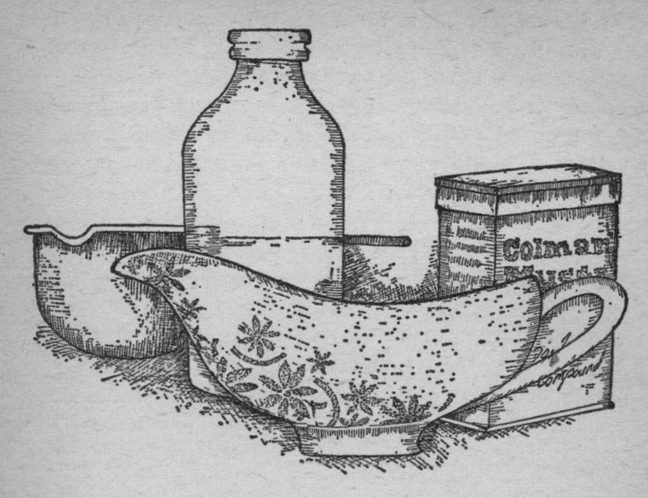

swollen (a process called cree-ing) and then simmered with milk, fruits and spices, and either eggs or brandy.

Frumenty was the most festive dish of all, served not only at Christmas but on all the other special days such as Mothering Sunday or Easter. It was also served at country fairs.

Frumenty looks very filling, but it is surprisingly light, as the wheat grains are so puffed up. The combination of flavours and textures is indescribable, but ambrosiac. You can serve it piping hot or leave it to cool so it is slightly set. It is the perfect Christmas breakfast – one wonders why it was ever forgotten.

The amounts below are enough for 8–10 people, but if you're not planning on a house party you can easily halve all the ingredients.

Frumenty

450 g (1 lb) wheat
water to cover
6 dl (1 pint) milk
100 g (4 oz) sultanas
100 g (4 oz) raisins
4 tablespoons honey
freshly grated nutmeg (about $\frac{1}{4}$ of a nut)
1 teaspoon ground cinnamon
4 tablespoons brandy
4 tablespoons double cream

Heat the oven to 110°C (225°F), Gas No. ¼.
Put the wheat into a large casserole and fill it to the brim with water. Cover it and put it into the oven for 12 hours. Take it out and let it stand until it is completely cool. Drain it in a colander in several batches. The grains will be soft, round and puffy. Put the wheat into a saucepan with the milk, sultanas, raisins, honey, nutmeg and cinnamon. Set it on a low heat, bring it to the boil and simmer, stirring frequently, until nearly all the liquid is absorbed. It will take 30–45 minutes. (If you want to prepare the frumenty in advance on Christmas Eve ready for the next morning, you can take it to this stage.) Take the pan from the heat and stir in the cream and brandy. (Or, if you prepared it in advance, leave it covered and than reheat it gently and then add the cream and brandy). If you want to serve it cold, pour it into a large dish and leave it in a cool place.

In some districts a similar dish was made with barley. It was flavoured only with nutmeg and called 'fluffin'.

Goose was for a long time the favourite poultry for the Christmas table, stuffed most probably with sage and onion and served with red cabbage. Afterwards there was Christmas pudding with brandy or rum butter, or perhaps a spiced apple or pumpkin pie. Then there would be the best of the summer's cheeses that had been sitting maturing in the cellar, accompanied by nuts, and rich wine or port.

Good breade and good drinke, a good fier in the hall,
Brawne, pudding and souse, and good mustard with all.
Beefe, mutton and porke, shred pies of the best,
Pig, veale, goose and capon, and turkey well drest;
Cheese, apples and nuts, joly Carols to heare,
And then in the countrie is counted good cheare.

Bibliography

Arnold, James, *The Shell Book of Country Crafts*, John Baker, 1968

Aylett, Mary, *Country Wines*, Odhams Press Ltd, 1953

Baker, Margaret, *Discovering the Folklore of Plants*, Shire Publications 1971

Bickerdyke, John, *The Curiosities of Ale and Beer*, first published 1889, Spring Books, 1965

Blakeborough, Richard, *Yorkshire Wit, Character, Folklore and Customs*, first published 1889, EP Publishing Ltd, 1973

Boase, Wendy, *The Folklore of Hampshire and the Isle of Wight*, B. T. Batsford Ltd, 1974

Briggs, Katherine, M., *The Folklore of the Cotswolds*, B. T. Batsford Ltd, 1974

Carruthers, F. J., *Lore of the Lake Country*, Robert Hale and Co, 1975

Clare, John, *The Shepherds Calendar*, Oxford Paperbacks, 1964

Cobbett, William, *Cobbett's Cottage Economy*, first published 1823, Landsman's Bookshop Ltd, 1974

Courtney, M. A., *Cornish Feasts and Folklore*, revised and reprinted from the Folk-Lore Society Journals 1886–7, EP Publishing Ltd, 1973

Culpeper, Nicholas, *Culpeper's Complete Herbal*, W. Foulsham and Co Ltd, London

Deane, Tony and Shaw, Tony, *The Folklore of Cornwall*, B. T. Batsford Ltd, 1974

Drive Publications Ltd, 1973, *The Readers Digest Book of the Countryside*

Ewart Evans, George, *The Farm and the Village*, Faber and Faber Ltd 1969

The Horse in the Furrow, Faber and Faber Ltd, 1960

Ask the Fellows Who Cut the Hay, Faber and Faber Ltd, 1956

The Pattern Under the Plough, Faber and Faber Ltd, 1966

Genders, Roy, *The Scented Wild Flowers of Britain*, Collins, 1971

Glyde Jnr., John, (Ed), *Folklore and Customs of Norfolk*, first published 1872, EP Publishing Ltd, 1973

Grieve, Mrs M., *A Modern Herbal*, Peregrine Books, 1976

Harley, Rev. Timothy, FRAS, *Moon Lore*, first published 1885, EP Publishing Ltd, 1973

Hartley, Dorothy, *Food in England*, Macdonald, 1973 edn.
Made in England, Methuen and Co Ltd, 1951 edn
edited by, *Thomas Tusser, His Good Points of Husbandry*, Country Life Ltd, 1931

Henderson, William, *Folklore of the Northern Counties of England and the Borders*, first published 1866, EP Publishing Ltd, 1973

Hewett, Sarah, *Nummits and Crummits*, first published 1900, EP Publishing Ltd, 1976

Hole, Christina, *Traditions and Customs of Cheshire*, first published 1937, SR publishing Ltd, 1970

Jewell, Brian, *Fairs and Revels*, Midas Books, 1976

Jones-Baker, Doris, *Old Hertfordshire Calendar*, Phillimore and Co Ltd, 1974

Leather, *Ella Mary*, *Folk-Lore of Herefordshire*, first published Hereford 1912, EP Publishing Ltd, 1973

Lewis, Don, *Curious and Humorous Customs*, A. R. Mowbray and Co Ltd, 1972

McNeil, F. Marian, *The Silver Bough, Vol 1, A Calendar of Scottish National Festivals*, William Maclellan, 1959

Newell, Venetia, *Discovering the Folklore of Birds and Beasts*, Shire Publications, 1971

Owen, Rev. Elias, *Welsh Folklore*, first published 1888, EP Publishing Ltd, 1976

Palaiseul, Jean, *Grandmother's Secrets*, Penguin Books, 1976

Palmer, Kingsley, *The Folklore of Somerset*, B. T. Batsford Ltd, 1976

Palmer, Roy, *The Folklore of Warwickshire*, B. T. Batsford Ltd, 1976

Porter, Enid, *The Folklore of East Anglia*, B. T. Batsford Ltd, 1974

Simpson, Jaqueline, *The Folklore of the Welsh Border*, B. T. Batsford Ltd, 1976

Soil Association Booklet, *Friend and Foe in the Garden*

Summerfield, Geoffrey, ed., *Voices, The Second Book*, Penguin Books Ltd, 1976

Tusser, Thomas, *Five Hundred Points of Good Husbandry*, James Tregaskis and Son, 1931

Uttley, Alison, *A Year in the Country*, Howard Baker Press Ltd, 1976

West Kent Federation of Women's Institutes, *Old Kentish Recipes, A 'Gestetner' Reproduction* by Mr A. E. Hockley, 9, Park Avenue, Deal, Kent. (Date unknown)

Whitlock, Ralph, *The Folklore of Devon*, B. T. Batsford Ltd, 1977

Wiltshire, Katharine, *The Folklore of Wiltshire*

Woodward, Marcus, arranged by, *Leaves from Gerard's Herbal*, Thorson's Publishers Ltd, Copyright The Bodley Head, 1927

Index

Alder 138
Ale and cheese 194
Animals, farm 32–48, 54–6
 and the weather 153
Ants 76
Apple 25–8
 pudding 208–9
Ash 136

Baby's first food 84
 gift for new 85
Bacon and onion pudding 181
Beauty, natural 113–17
Bedroom 78
Beech 138
Beekeeping 56–64
 hive 57
 stings 109
 swarming 60–1
 telling 59
Beer, home-made 164–71
Birch 140
Bird scaring 19–20
Birth 82–5
 marks 85
 predicting 82
Bites, insect 109
Blackthorn 145
Blossom 26
Boxwood 146
Brawn, festive 214
Bread baking 157–60, 208
Breakages 75
Bruises 109–10
Building 65
Burns and scalds 110
Butter 51–2

Calendar, weather 148–50
Calving 43
Carlins 188
Cattle 41–4
 calving 43
 cowmuck 44
 cowshed 43
Chapped hands 108
 lips and nose 108
Cheese 52–4
 and ale 194
Chicken pie 179–80
 and parsley pie 200
Chickens 54–5
Chilblains 111–12
Childbirth 82–3
Childcare 85
Cider 160–4
Clare, John 13
Cleaning 73
Clothes 81–2
 mending 81
Cold remedy 120–1
Compost heap 96–9
Cornish heavy cake 196
Corns 112
Cough 96–9
Courting 88
Cowmuck 44
Cowshed 43
Cramp 105
Crinkling cake 212

Crop colour 24
rotation 17
and weather 20–2
Curd tart 198
Curds and whey 194
Cuts and grazes 110

Dairy 43–54
butter 52
cheese 52–4
milk 51
milking 49–50
Death 91–4
omens 91–3
Dogwood 145–6
Ducks 55–6
Dyeing 80–1
wool 81

Earache 108
Easter cakes 192
Elder 144
Elm 139

Farm 15
animals 32–48, 54–6
Farmer's wife 88
Farming, mixed 15
Festive brawn 214
Figgey pudding 188–9
Fire 71
Fleas 76
Flies 76
Food, baby's first 84
Fruit 26–7
blossom 26
harvest 27–8
soft 130–1
storing 25
Frumenty 216–17

Garden, country 134
pests 131–4

Geese 56
eggs baked 191
Gift for new baby 85
Gingerbread men 199–200
Gooseberry tart 194–5
Grafting 26
Grazes 110

Hair care 114
Hands, care of 116
chapped 108
Harvest 23–5
fruit 27–8
wheat 23
Hawthorn 136–7
Haymaking 22–3
Hazel 141–2
water rod 142
Headaches 102–3
Hearth 70
Herbs 126–30
drying 129–30
Hiccoughs 104
Hiring servants 75
Honey 63
Hops 28–32
drying 31
in home brewing 166
picking 30–1
poles and wires 29
stringing 29–30
Hornbeam 144
Horses 44–8
brasses 47–8
gelding 46
Hot cross buns 190
Household pests 76–7

Indigestion 103–4
Influenza 101–2
Insect bites 109
Insomnia 103
Insulation 65–6

Labour pain 82
Lambing 39–40
Lard 211 12
Lardy cake 213
Lightning 67–8
Lighting 72–3
Lime 143
Linens 78–9
 washing 79
Lips, chapped 108
Love 86–91

Malt 166
Marriage 86–91
Mattress filling 78
Milk 51
Milking 49–50
Mixed farming 15
Moon and the weather 152–3
Mothering Sunday 185–6
Moving house 70
Mushrooms, pickled 210–11
Mustard sauce 215
Mutton pie 197–8

Natural beauty 113–17
 remedies 95–113
Nectar 62
Neuralgia 107
Nose, chapped 108

Oak 135–6
Oastcakes 204
Oat cakes 209–10
Onion and bacon pie 181

Painting 67
Pears 25–8
Pests, garden 131–4
 household 76–7
Pickled mushrooms 210–11
Pigs 33–6
Planting 17
Ploughing 16
 song 16
Plum cake, rich 193
 pudding 202
Polishing 73
Pomander 77
Pork, to salt 197
 soused shoulder 214–15
Potatoes 125
Poultry 54–6
Pruning 26
Pudding pie 184–5

Rabbit pudding 203
 raised pie with prunes 205
Rain 27
Remedies, natural 95–113
Rheumatism 106
Rich plum cake 193
 pudding 202
Ring, wedding 90
Rotation of crops 17
Rowan 144
Rush lighting 73

Salt beef in ale 204
 pork 197
Scab 27
Scalds 110
Sciatica 107
Seed cake 206
Servants, hiring 75
Sex, predicting baby's 82, 84
Sheep 36–41
 breeding 39
 counting 36–7
 feeding 38
 hurdles 37
 lambing 39–40
 marking 38
 shearing 38–9
 tail docking 40–1
 weaning 40

Simnel cake 186–7
Sky and the weather 150–1
Smells 77
Sneezing 99
Soil 17
  enriching 121
Song, ploughing 16
Sorrel sauce 19
Soused pork shoulder 214
Sowing crops 17
  vegetables 124–5
Spindle tree 143
Splinters 108
Sprains 111
Stars and the weather 152–3
Stings, bee and wasp 109
  nettle 108–9
Stomach upset 105
Storing fruit 28
Swarming 60–1
Sweeping 73–5
Sweet chestnut 147
Sycamore 143

Tail docking 40–1
Teeth 117
Thatching 66–7
Threshold 91
Tobacco 117–19
Toothache 107
Trees 134–47
  felling 146–7
  and the weather 154
Tusser, Thomas 13

Upset stomach 105

Valentine buns 182–3
Vegetables 122–6
  sowing 124–5

Walnut 141
Warts 112–13
Washing 79
Wasp sting 109
Wassailing 178–9
Water diviner 142
Wayfaring tree 145
Weaning 40
Weather 148–56
  calendar 148–50
  and crops 20–2
  moon, stars and 152–3
  signs from animals 153
  and sky 150–1
  trees, plants and 154
Wedding dress 90
  guests 91
  ring 90
Wheat 23–5
  harvest 23
Whooping cough 100–1
Wigs 183–4
Willow 140
Wind 150
Wines, country 171–6
Witches 45, 68–9
Wool dye 81

Yeast, bread 158
  brewing 167
Yew 137
Young, Arthur 13